AF411872

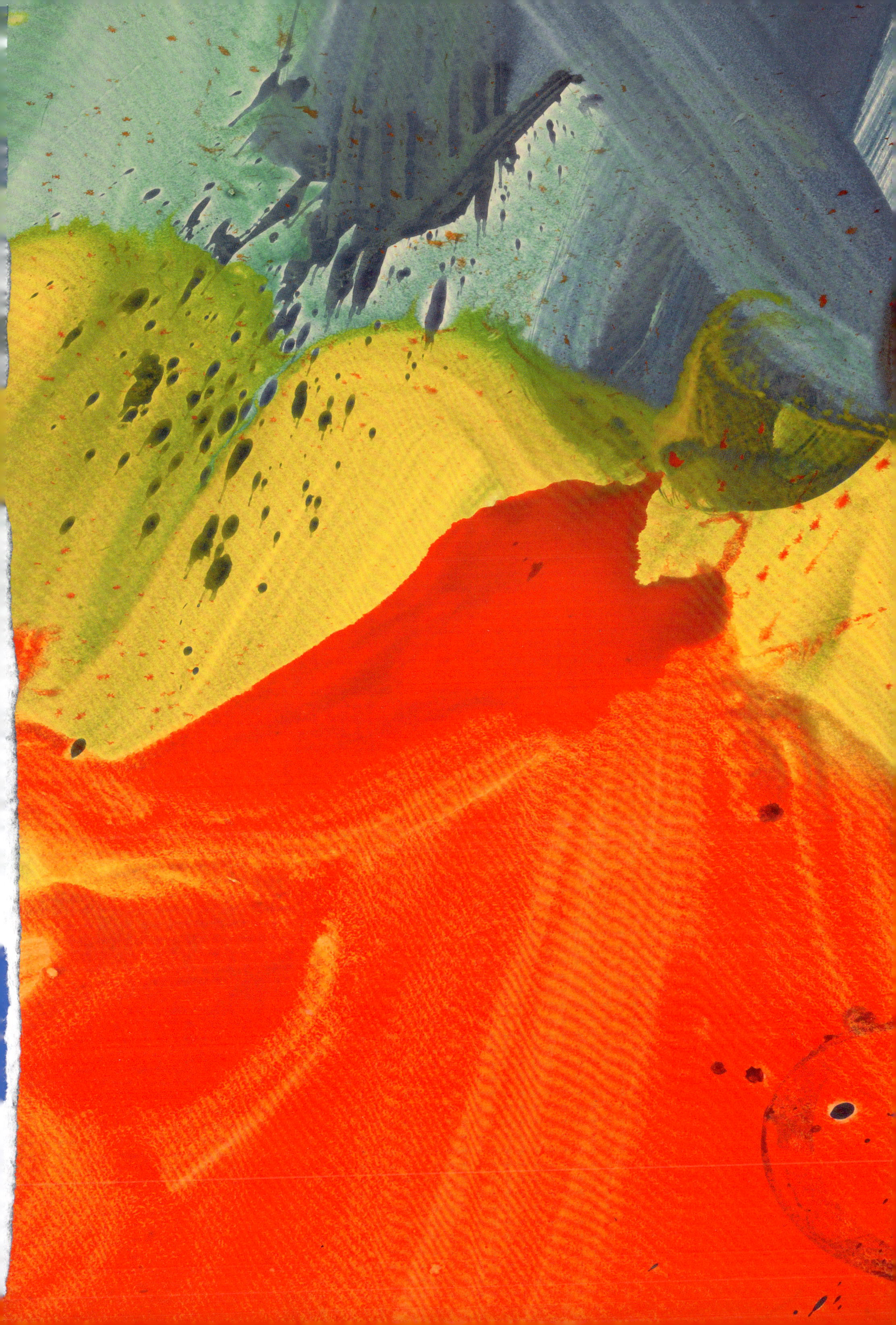

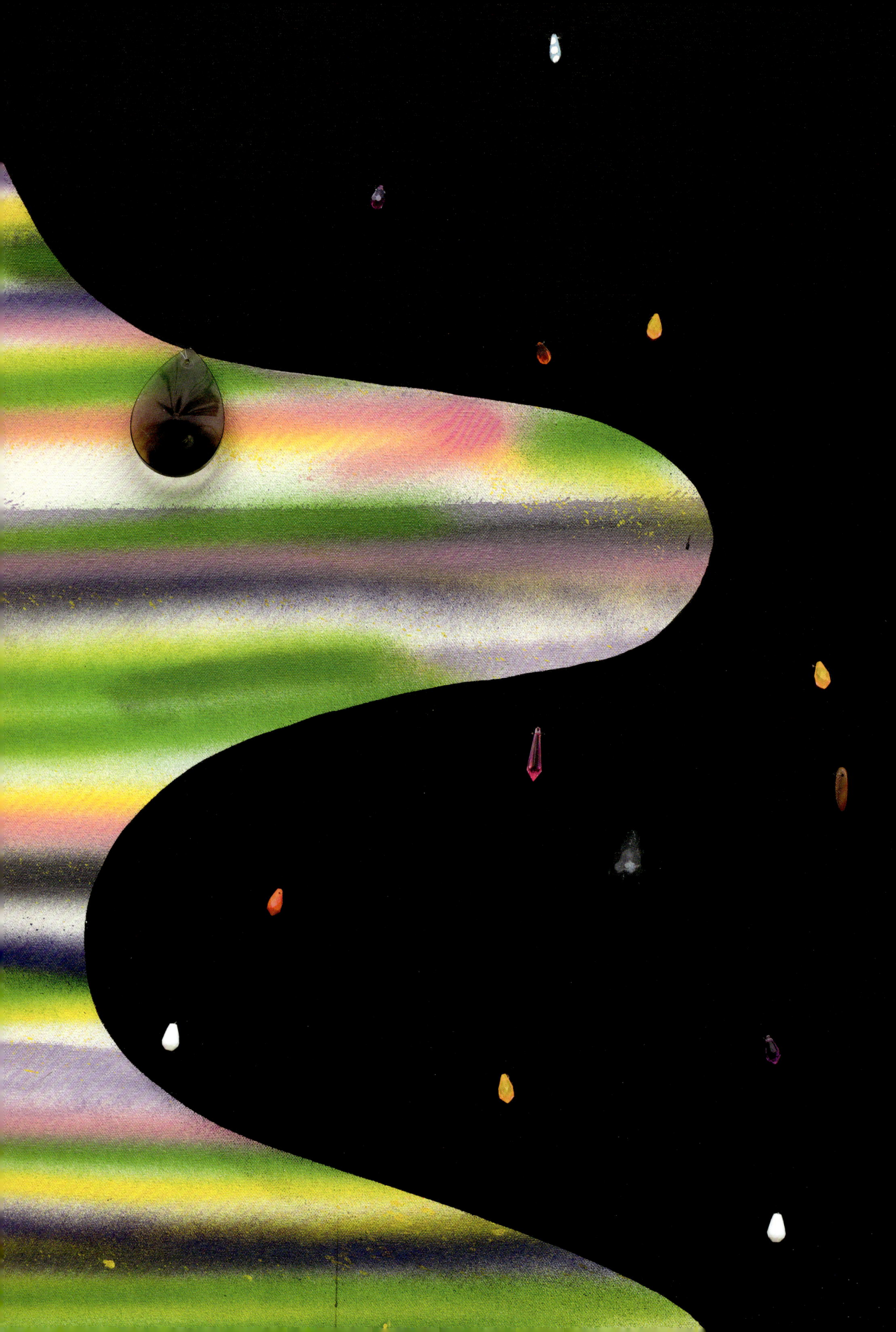

SARAH CAIN

ENTER THE CENTER

Ian Berry
with texts by
Andy Campbell, Lauren Haynes,
and Bernadette Mayer

The Frances Young
Tang Teaching Museum and Art Gallery
at Skidmore College
DelMonico Books · D.A.P.

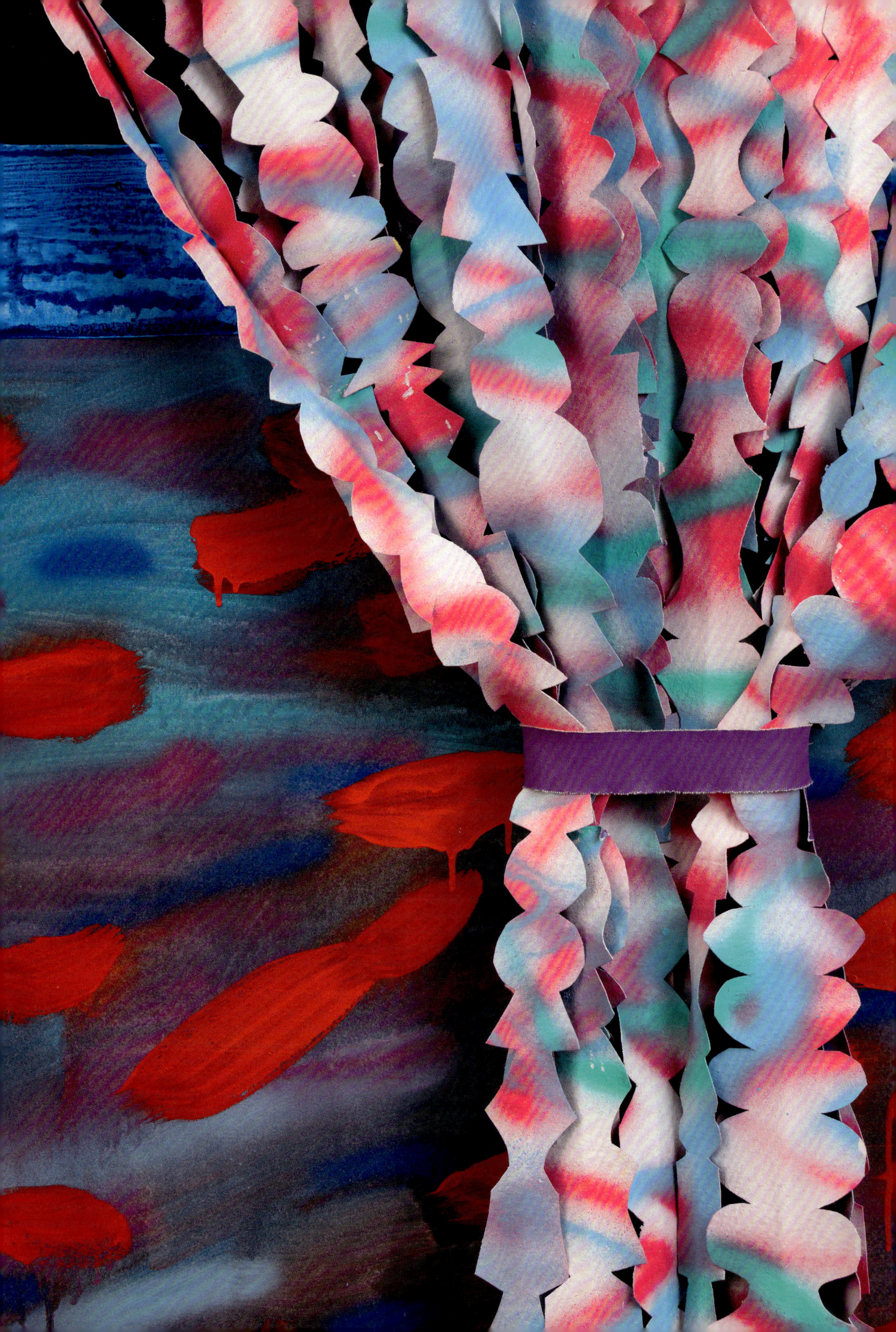

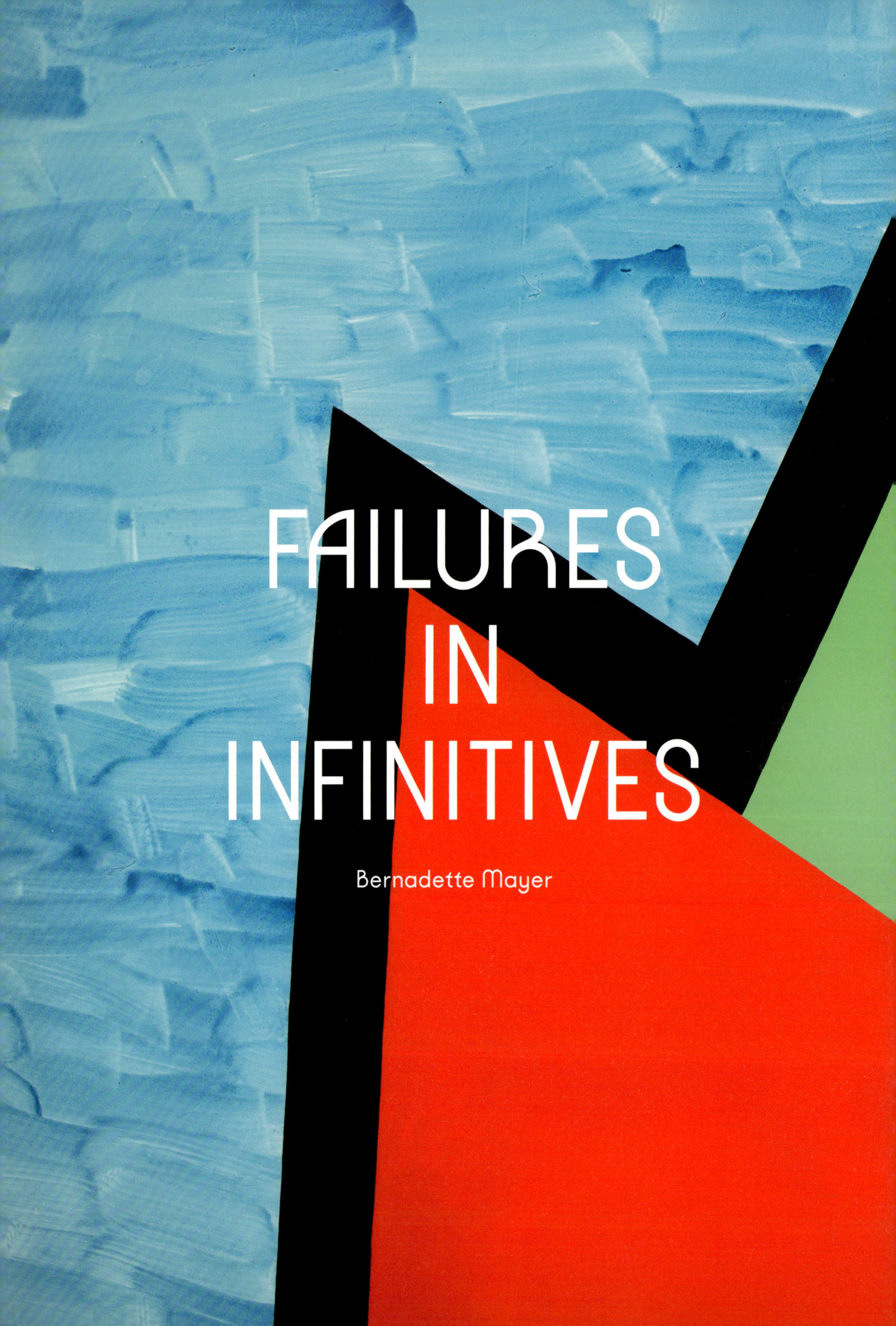
FAILURES
IN
INFINITIVES
Bernadette Mayer

why am i doing this? Failure
to keep my work in order so as
to be able to find things
to paint the house
to earn enough money to live on
to reorganize the house so as
to be able to paint the house &
to be able to find things and
earn enough money so as
to be able to put books together
to publish works and books
to have time
to answer mail & phone calls
to wash the windows
to make the kitchen better to work in
to have the money to buy a simple radio
to listen to while working in the kitchen
to know enough to do grownups work in the world
to transcend my attitude
to an enforced poverty
to be able to expect my checks
to arrive on time in the mail
to not always expect that they will not
to forget my mother's attitudes on humility or
to continue
to assume them without suffering
to forget how my mother taunted my father
about money, my sister about i cant say it
failure to forget mother and father enough
to be older, to forget them
to forget my obsessive uncle
to remember them some other way
to remember their bigotry accurately
to cease to dream about lions which always is
to dream about them, I put my hand in the lion's mouth
to assuage its anger, this is not a failure
to notice that's how they were; failure
to repot the plants
to be neat
to create & maintain clear surfaces
to let a couch or a chair be a place for sitting down
and not a table
to let a table be a place for eating & not a desk

to listen to more popular music
to learn the lyrics
to not need money so as
to be able to write all the time
to not have to pay rent, con ed or telephone bills
to forget parents' and uncle's early deaths so as
to be free of expecting care; failure
to love objects
to find them valuable in any way; failure
to preserve objects
to buy them and
to now let them fall by the wayside; failure
to think of poems as objects
to think of the body as an object; failure
to believe; failure
to know nothing; failure
to know everything; failure
to remember how to spell failure; failure
to believe the dictionary & that there is anything
to teach; failure
to teach properly; failure
to believe in teaching
to just think that everybody knows everything
which is not my failure; I know everyone does; failure
to see not everyone believes this knowing and
to think we cannot last till the success of knowing
to wash all the dishes only takes ten minutes
to write a thousand poems in an hour
to do an epic, open the unwashed window
to let in you know who and
to spirit thoughts and poems away from concerns
to just let us know, we will
to paint your ceilings & walls for free

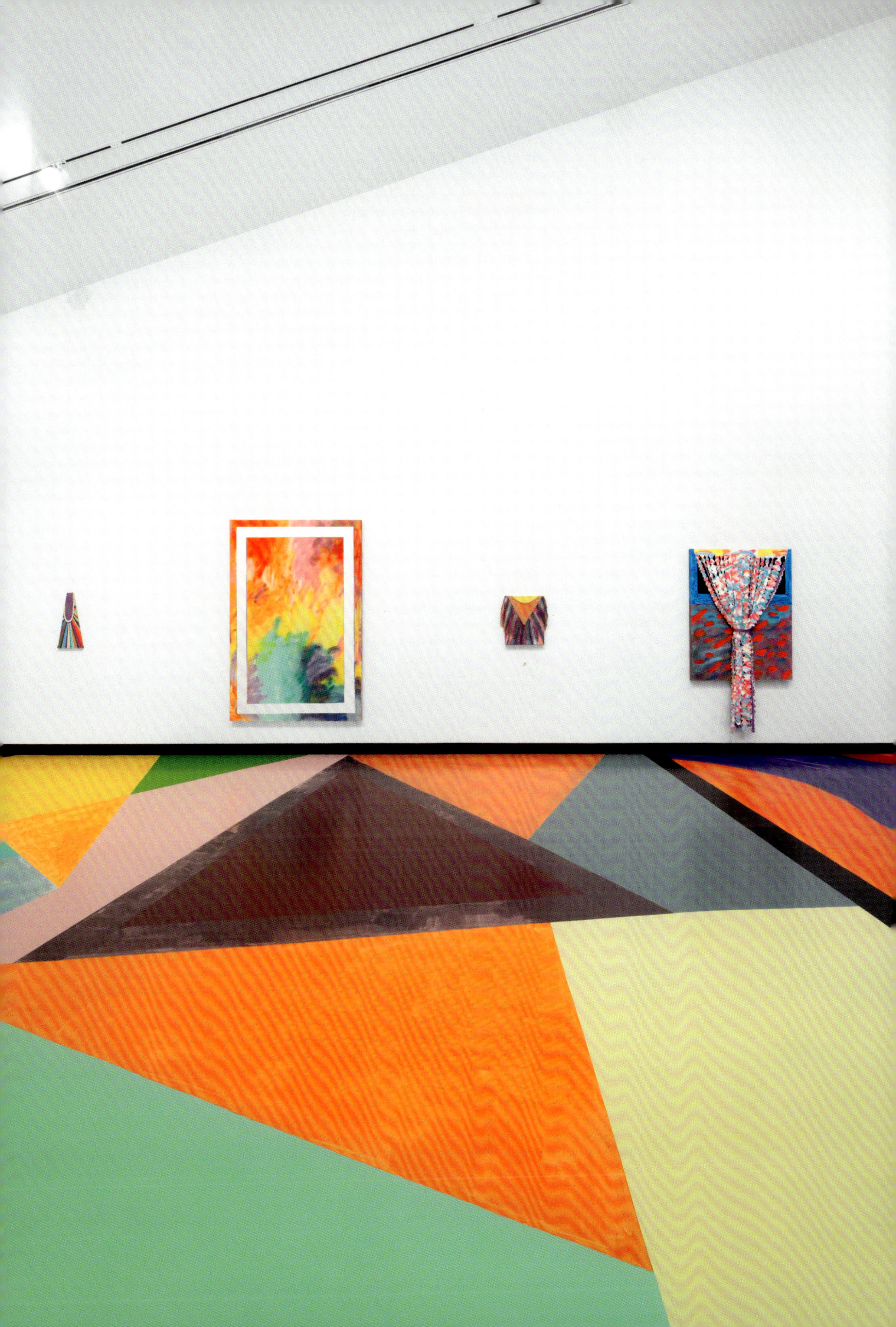

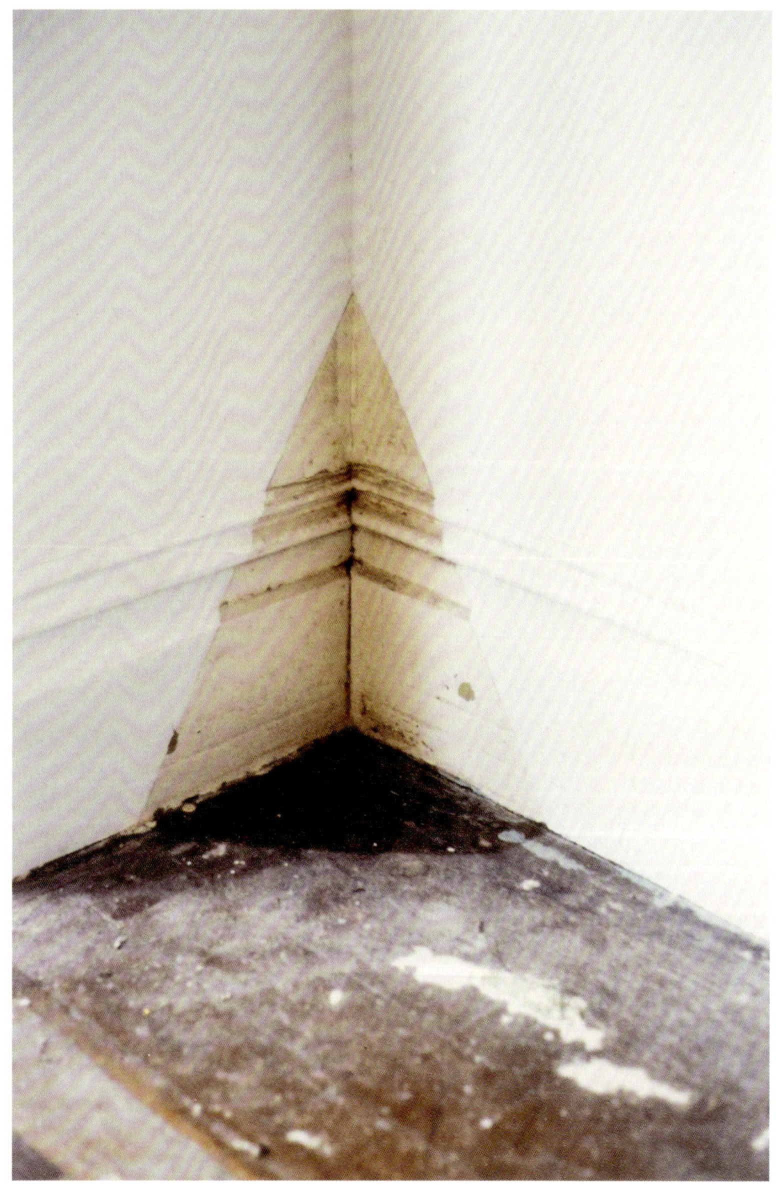

the alchemy of closeness, 2004

facing, **As You Continue To Walk Forward**, 2008

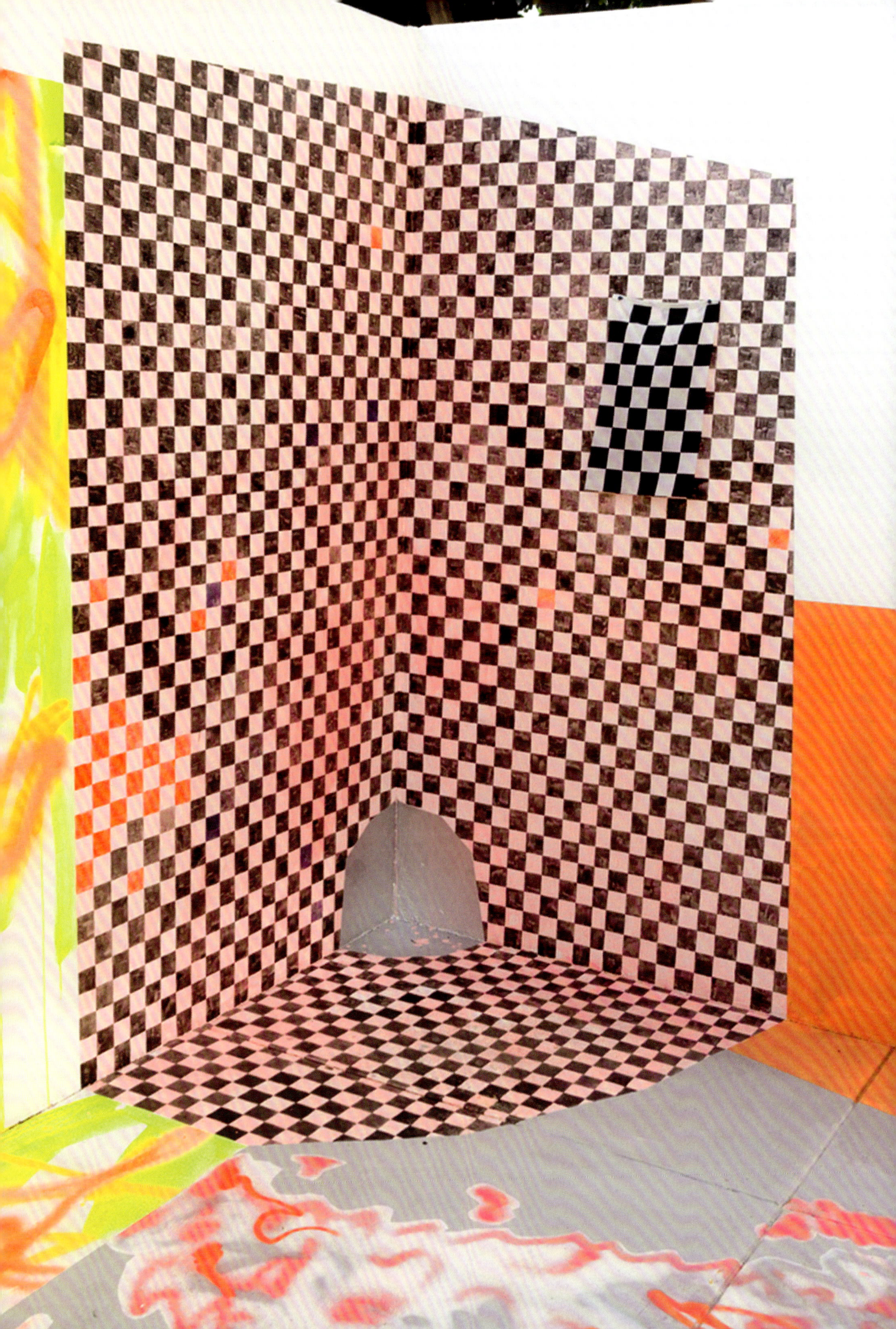

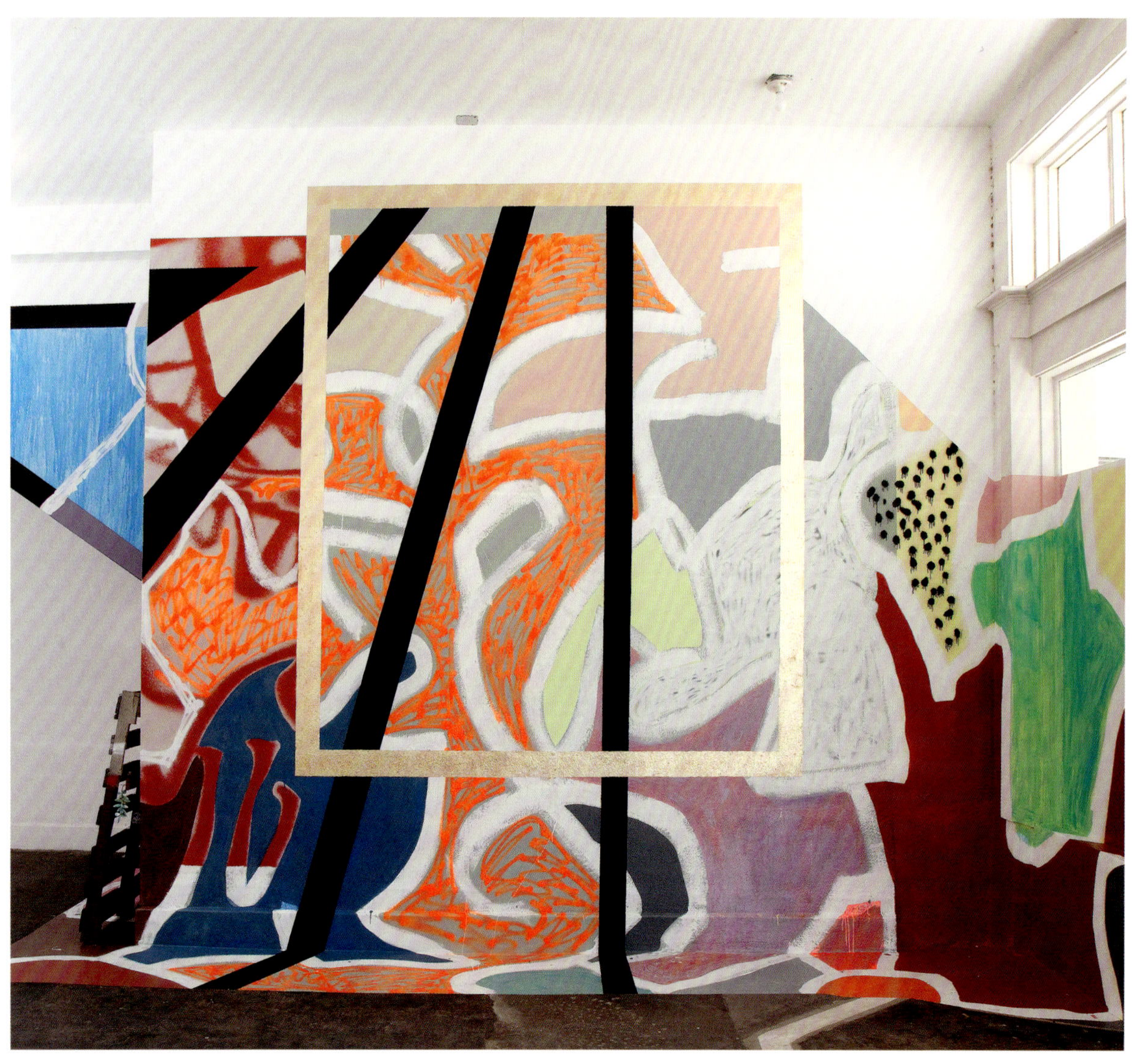

the face of satan, 2011

facing, **three, four, eight pm**, 2011
Installation view, Marfa, Texas

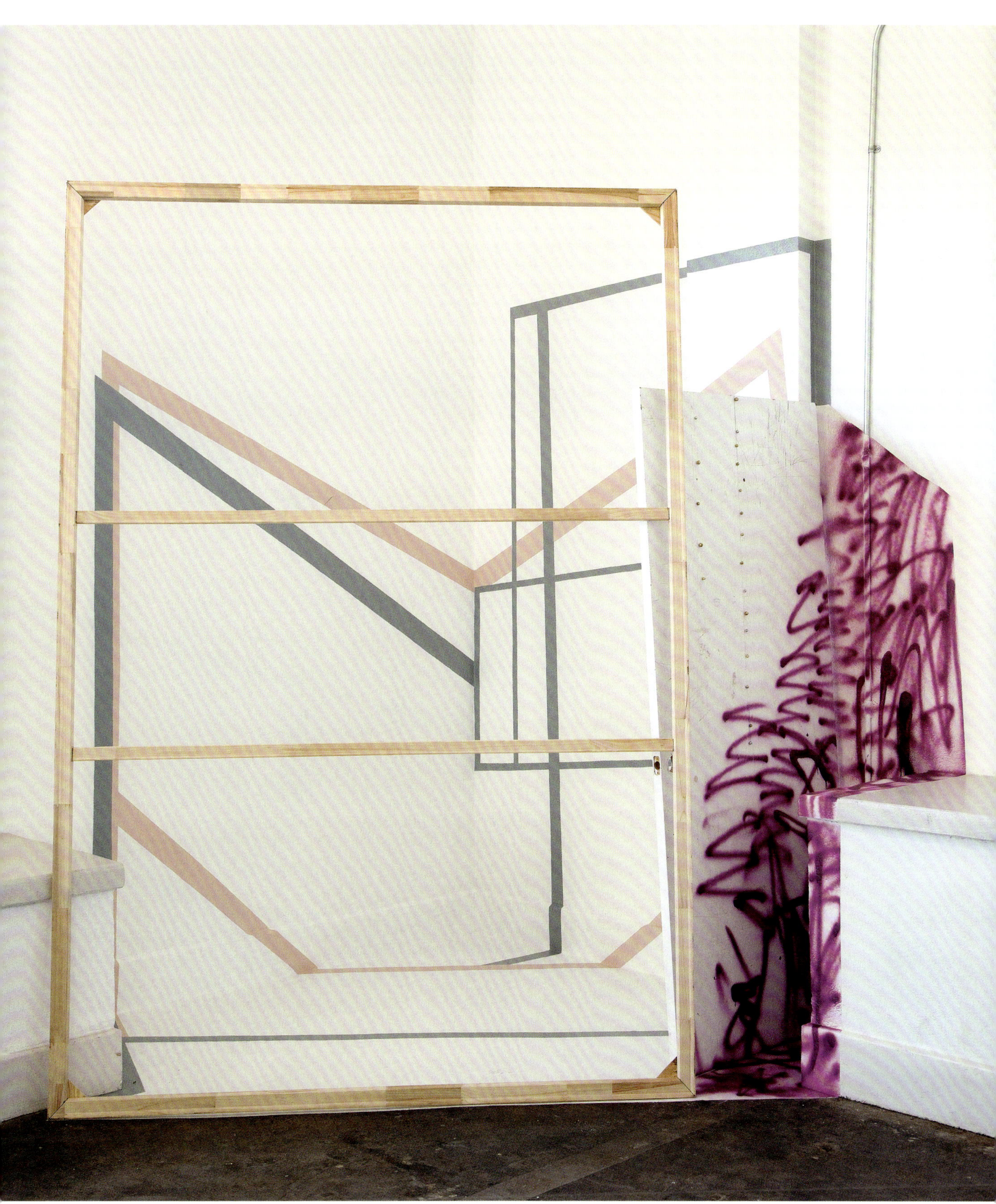

And the night never ended, 2018

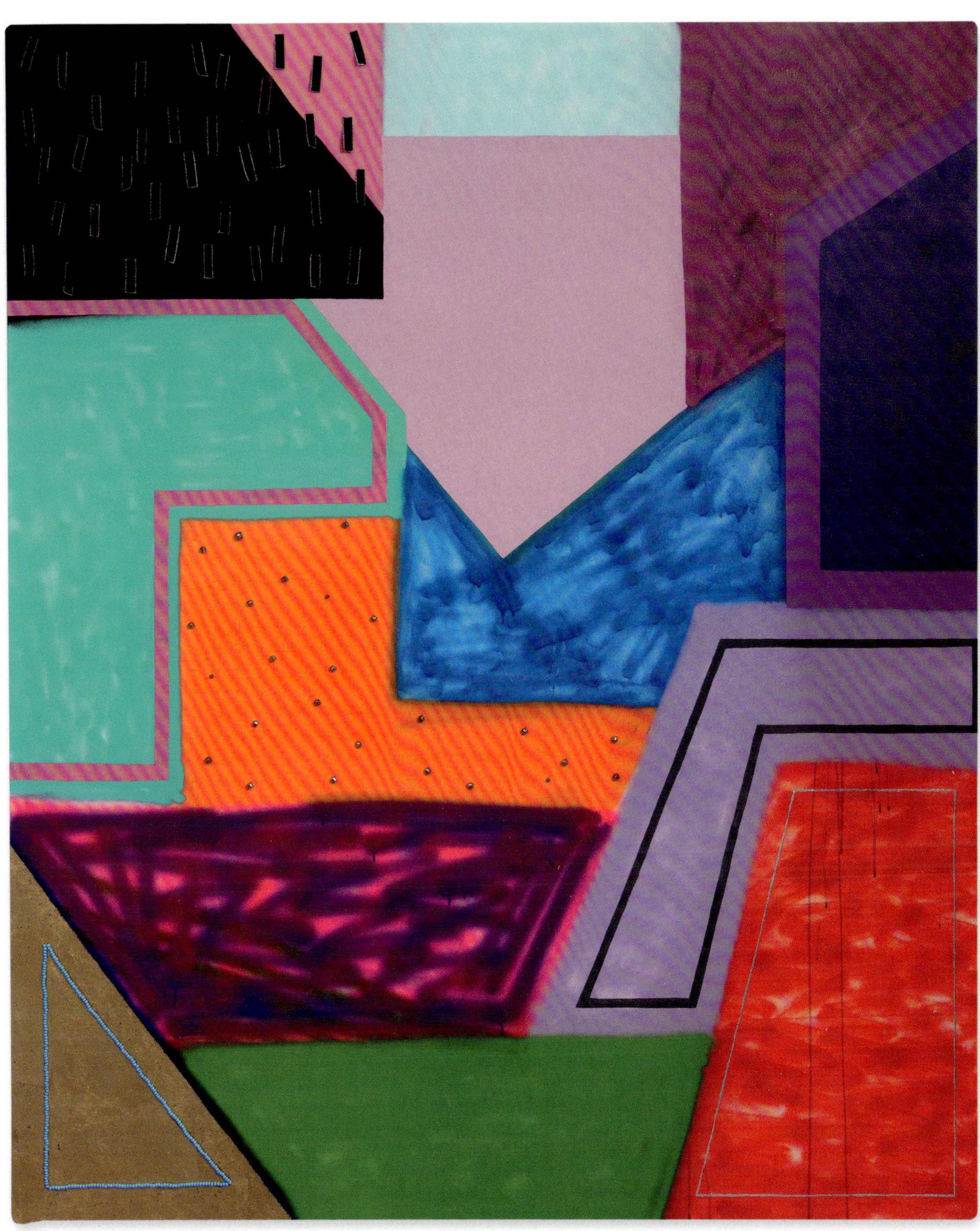

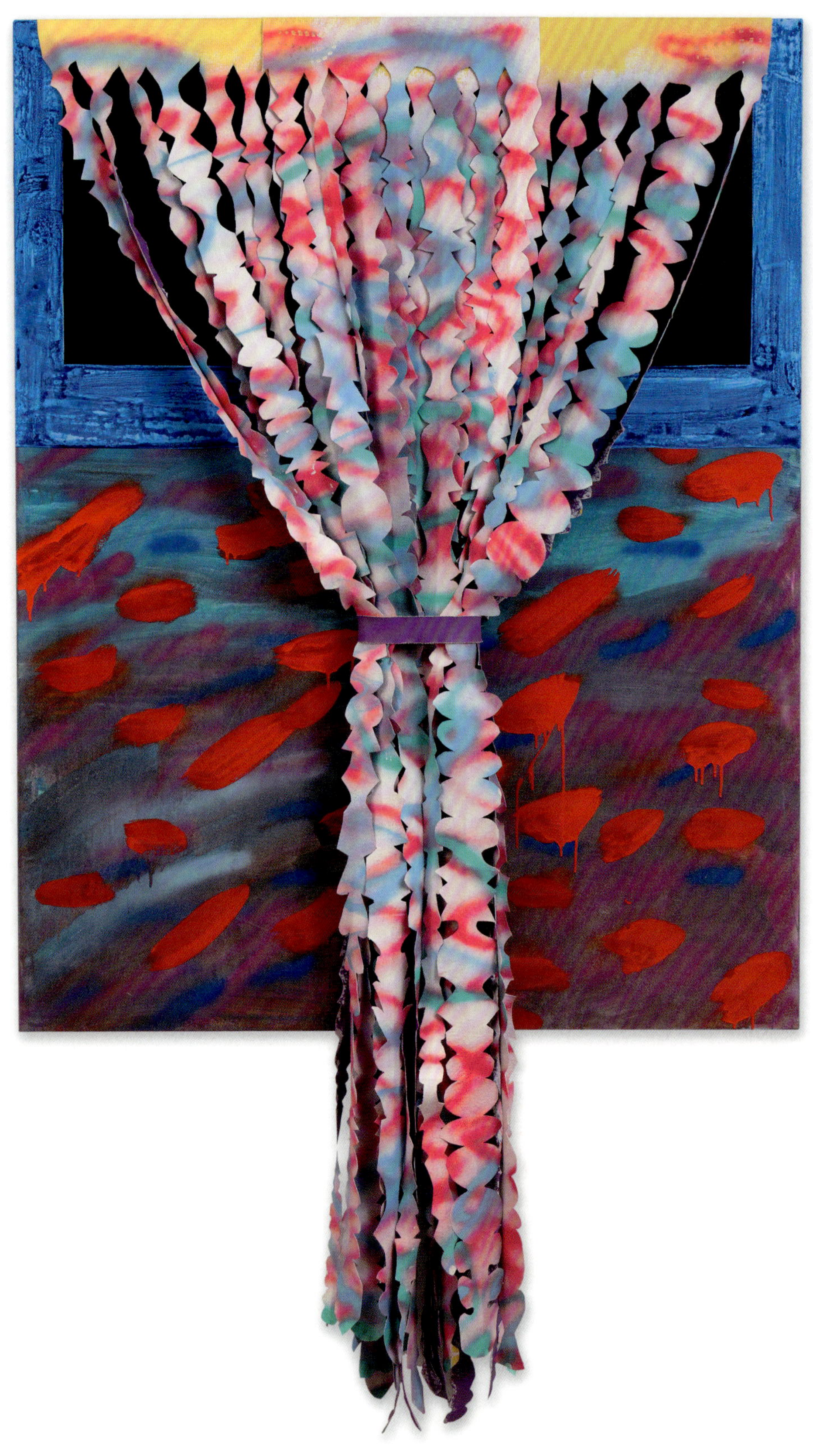

Martha, 2018

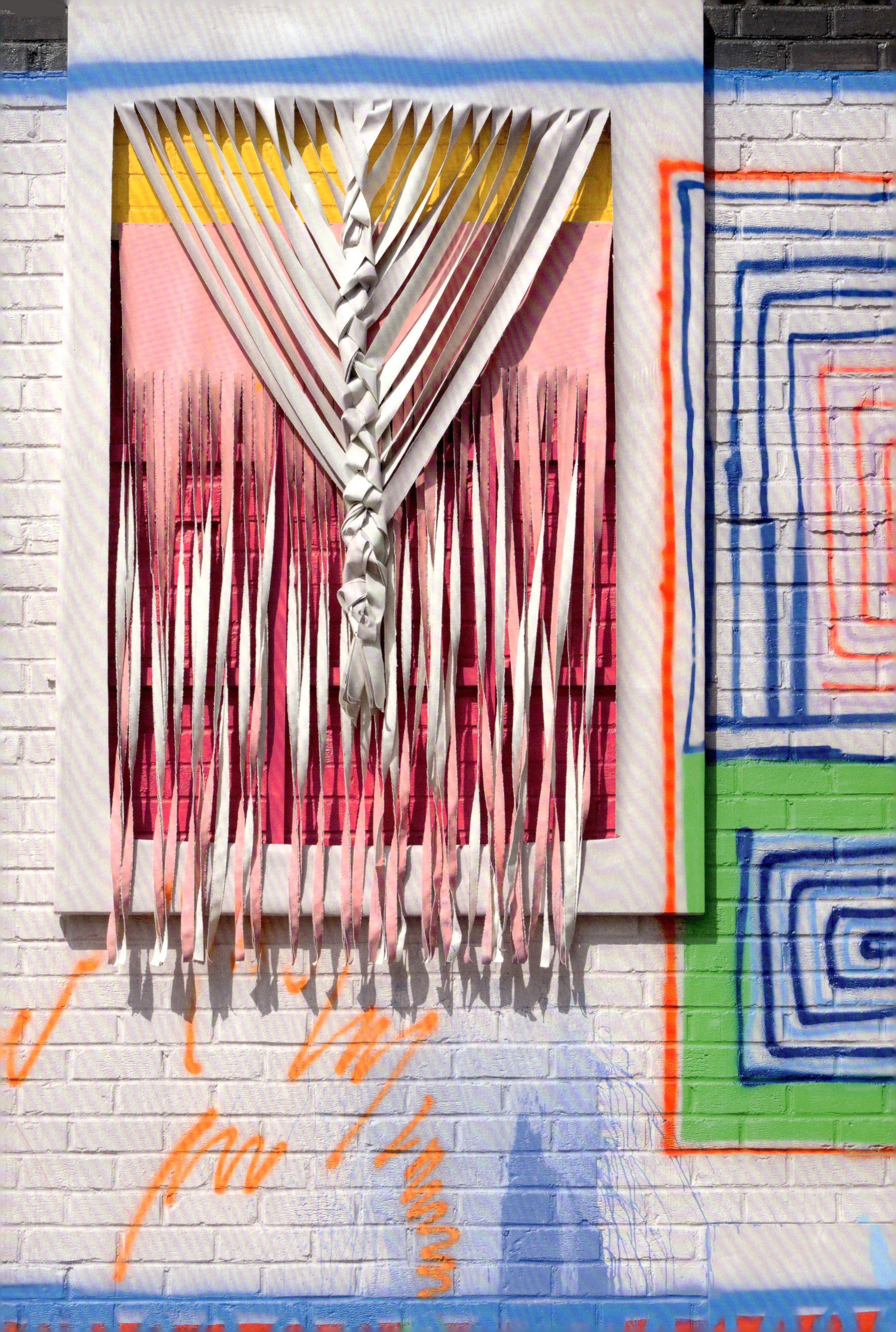

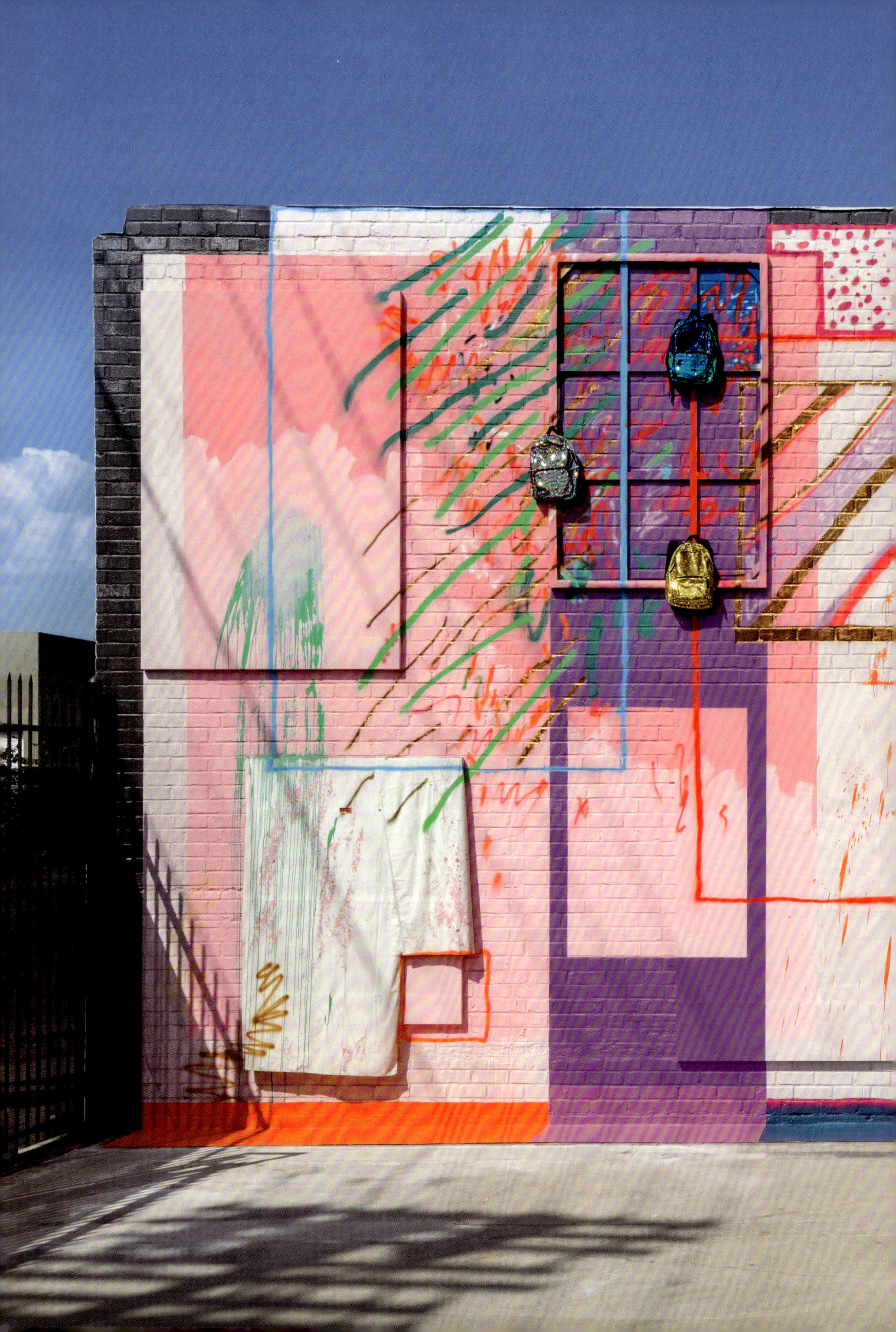

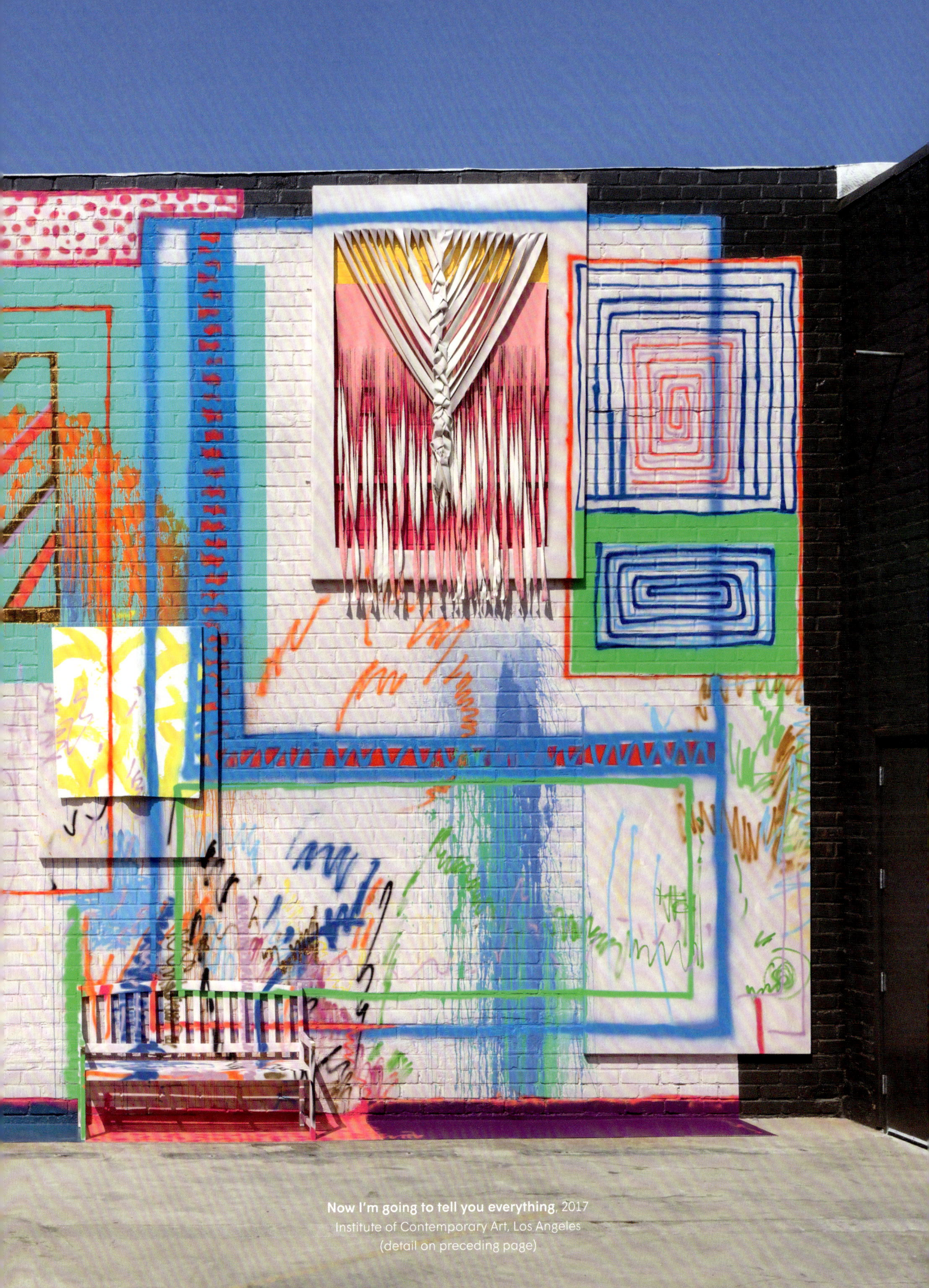

Now I'm going to tell you everything, 2017
Institute of Contemporary Art, Los Angeles
(detail on preceding page)

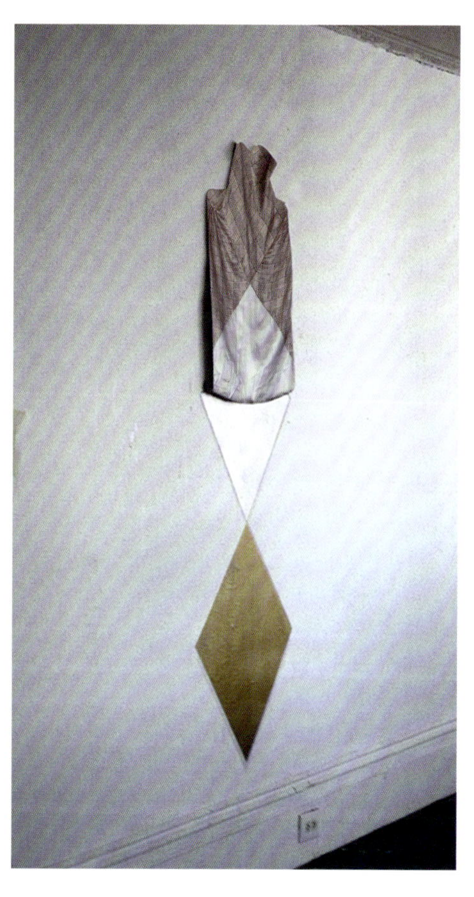 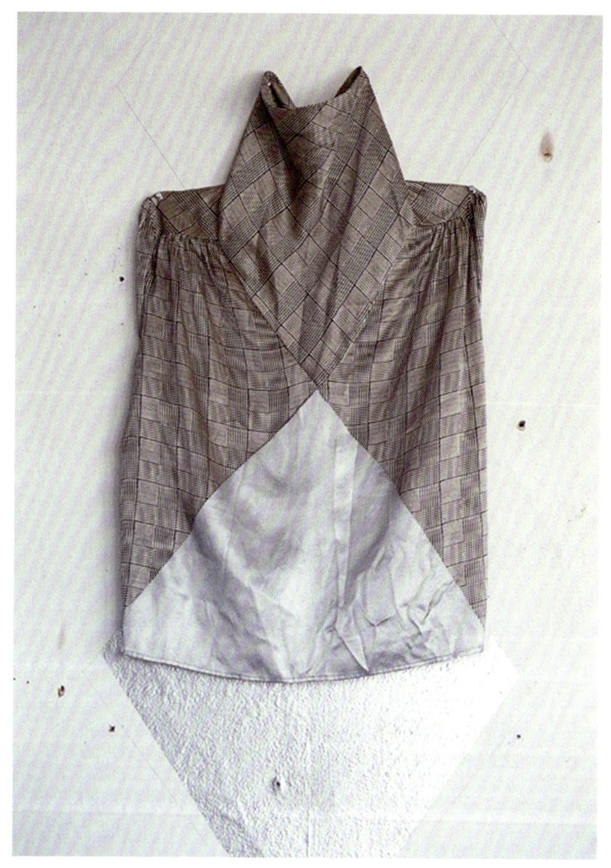

heavenly light (shirt), 2003

facing, **Untitled (Sister)**, 2006

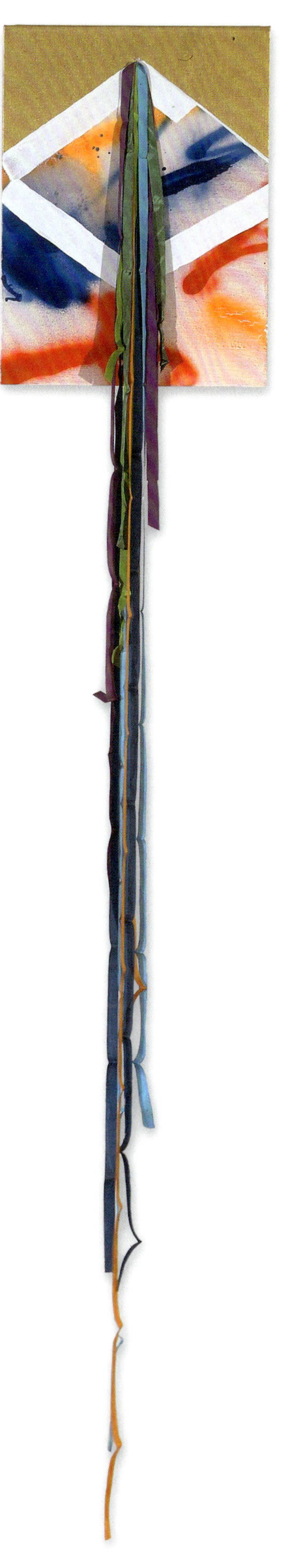

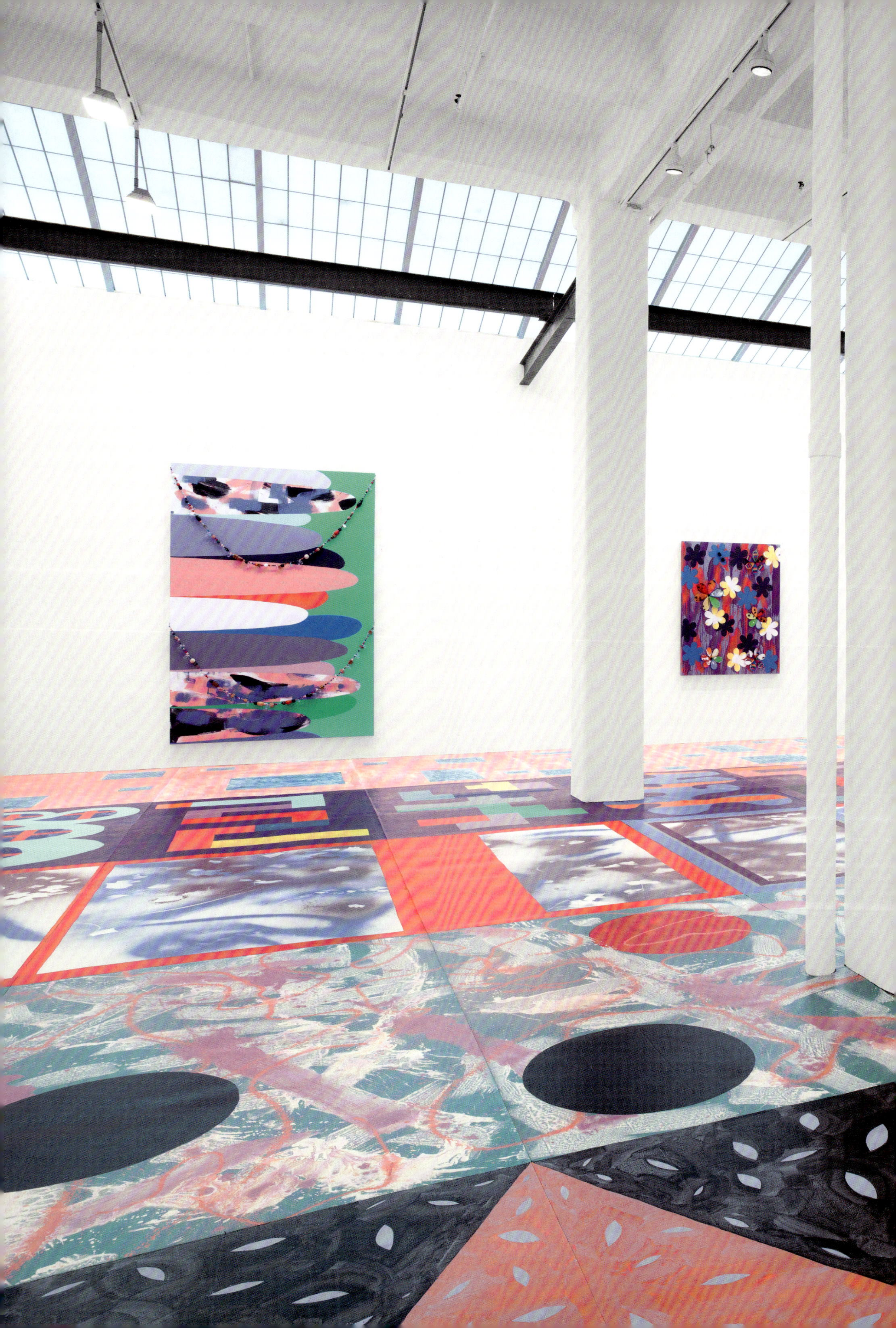

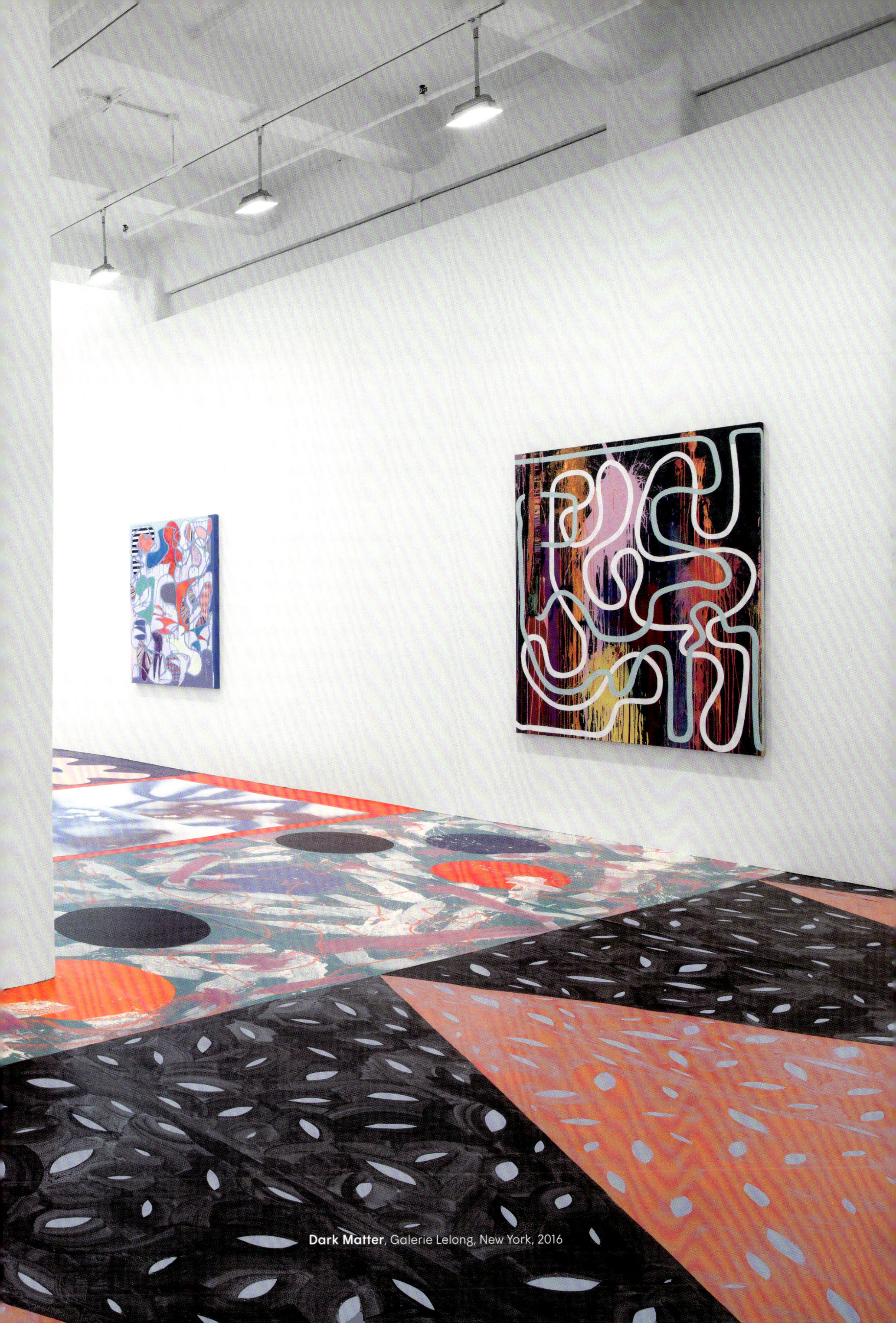

Dark Matter, Galerie Lelong, New York, 2016

Self Portrait, 2018

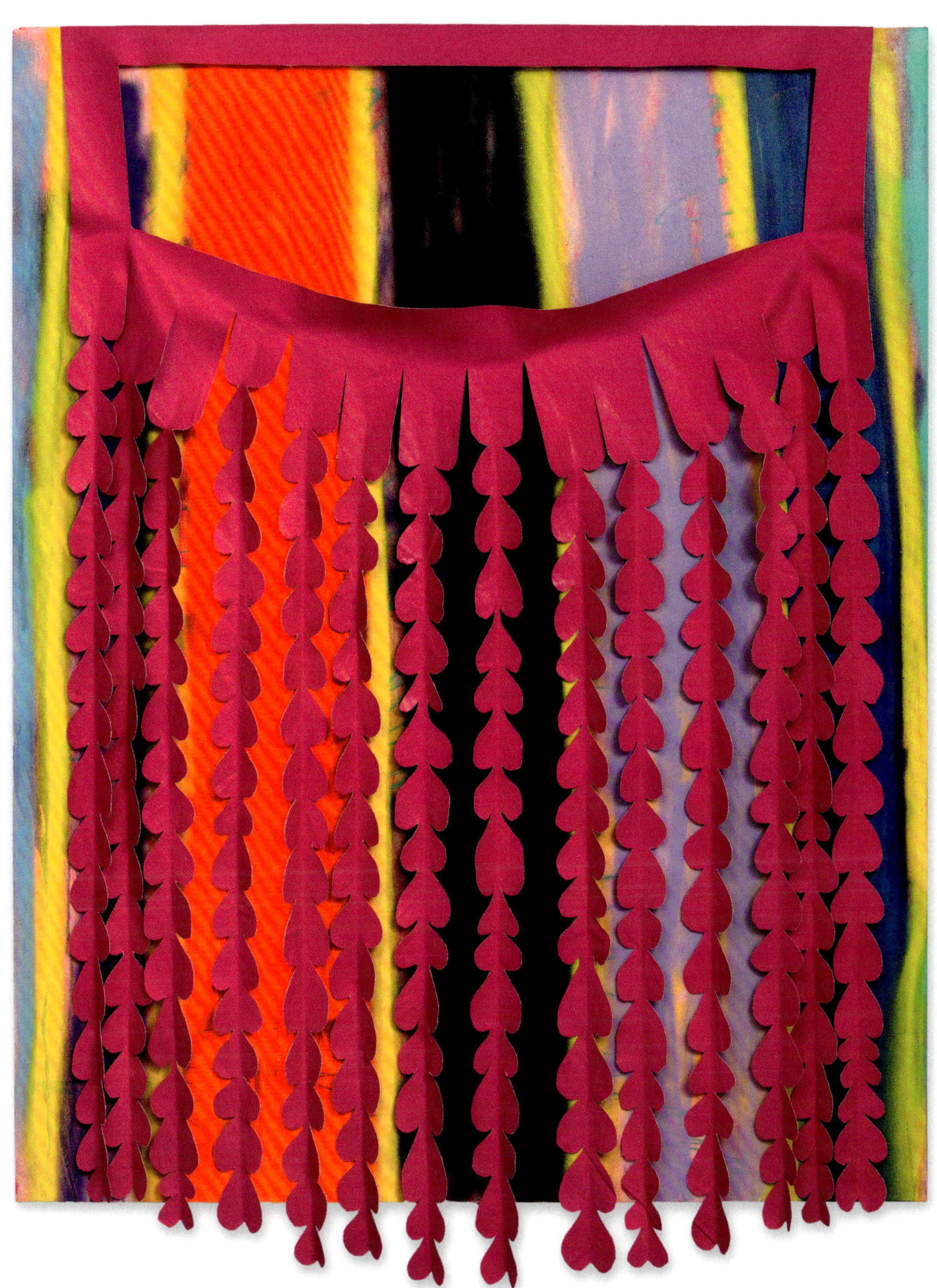

Self Portrait, 2018

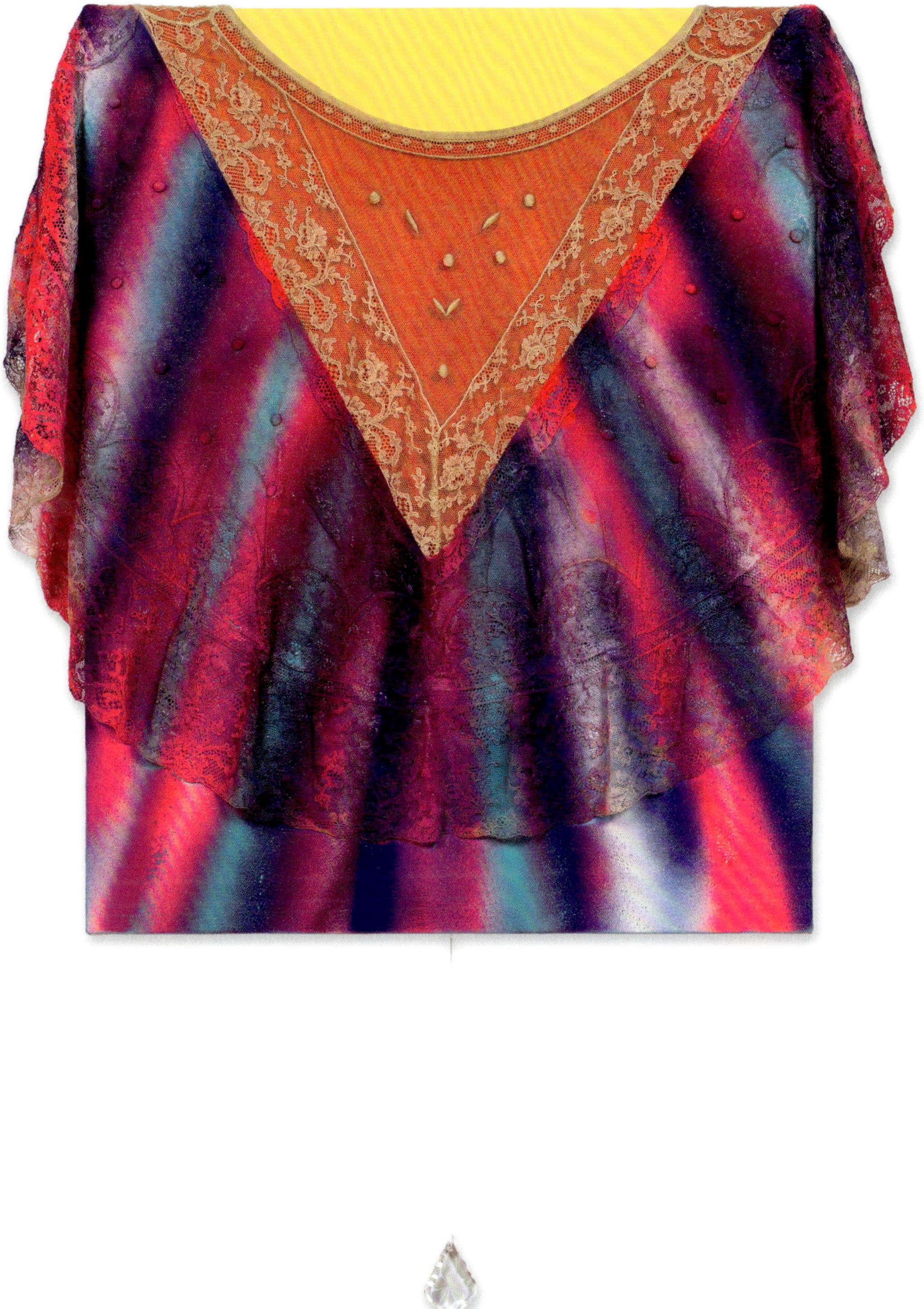

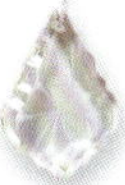

Black Magic, 2016

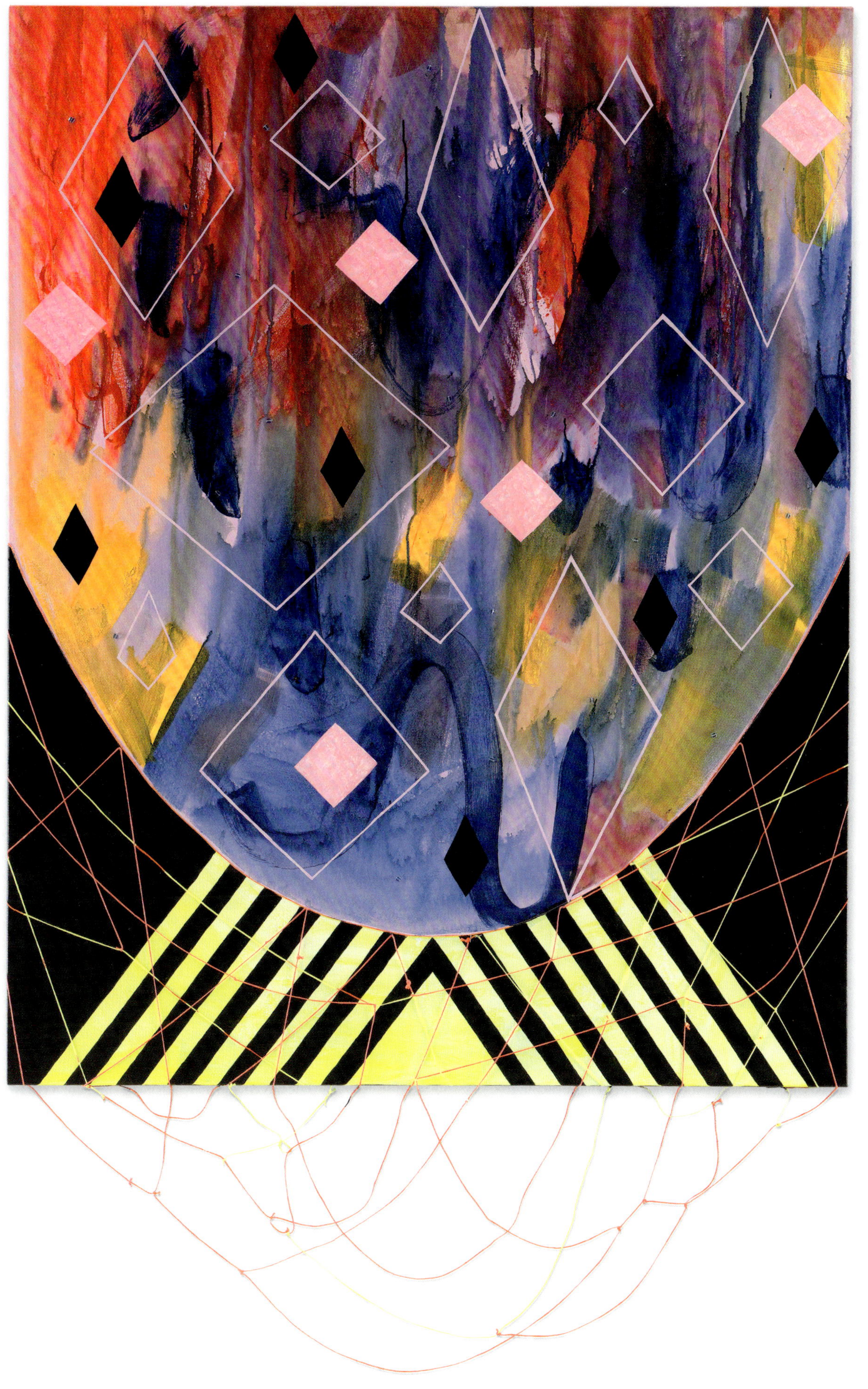

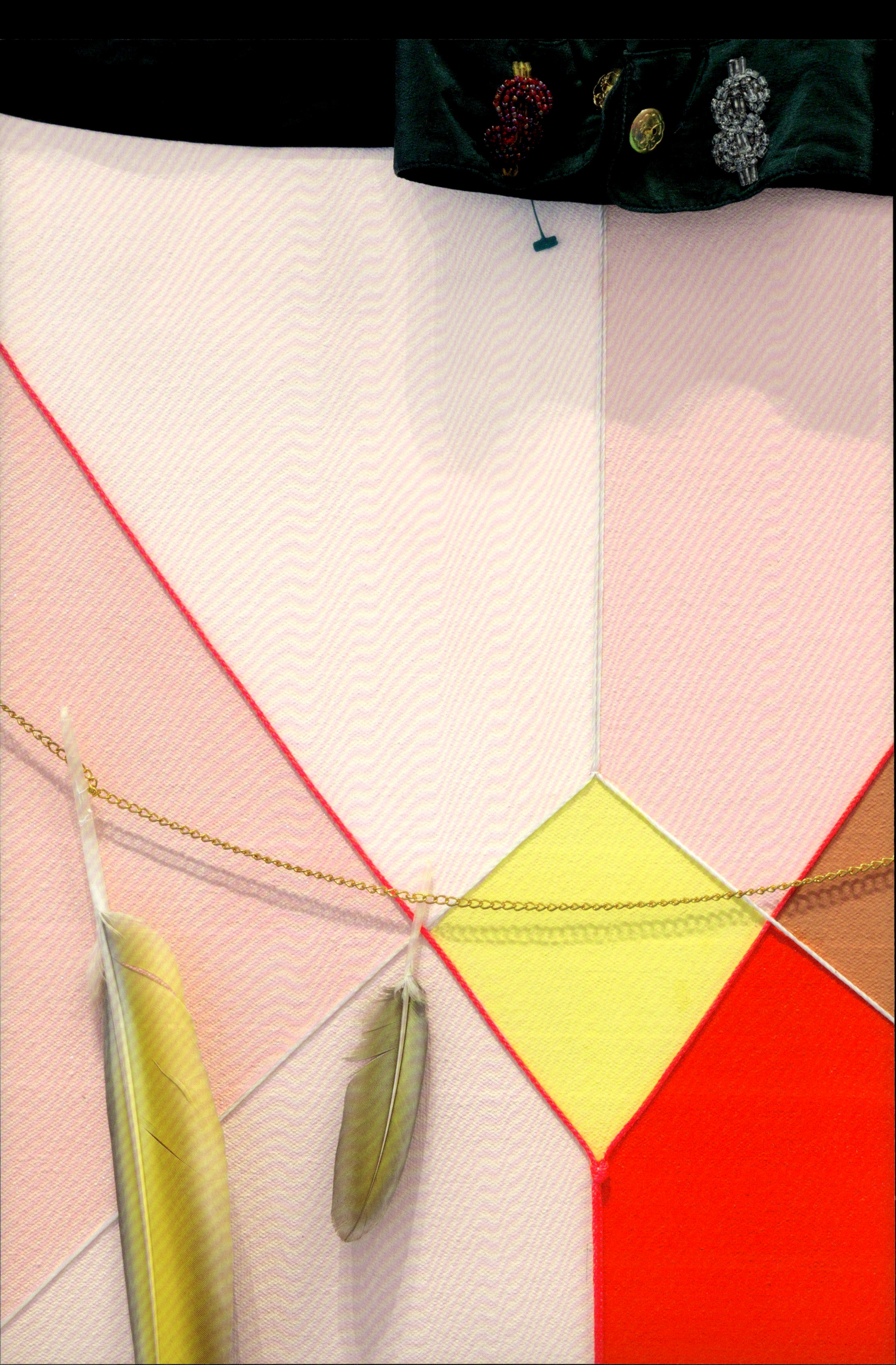

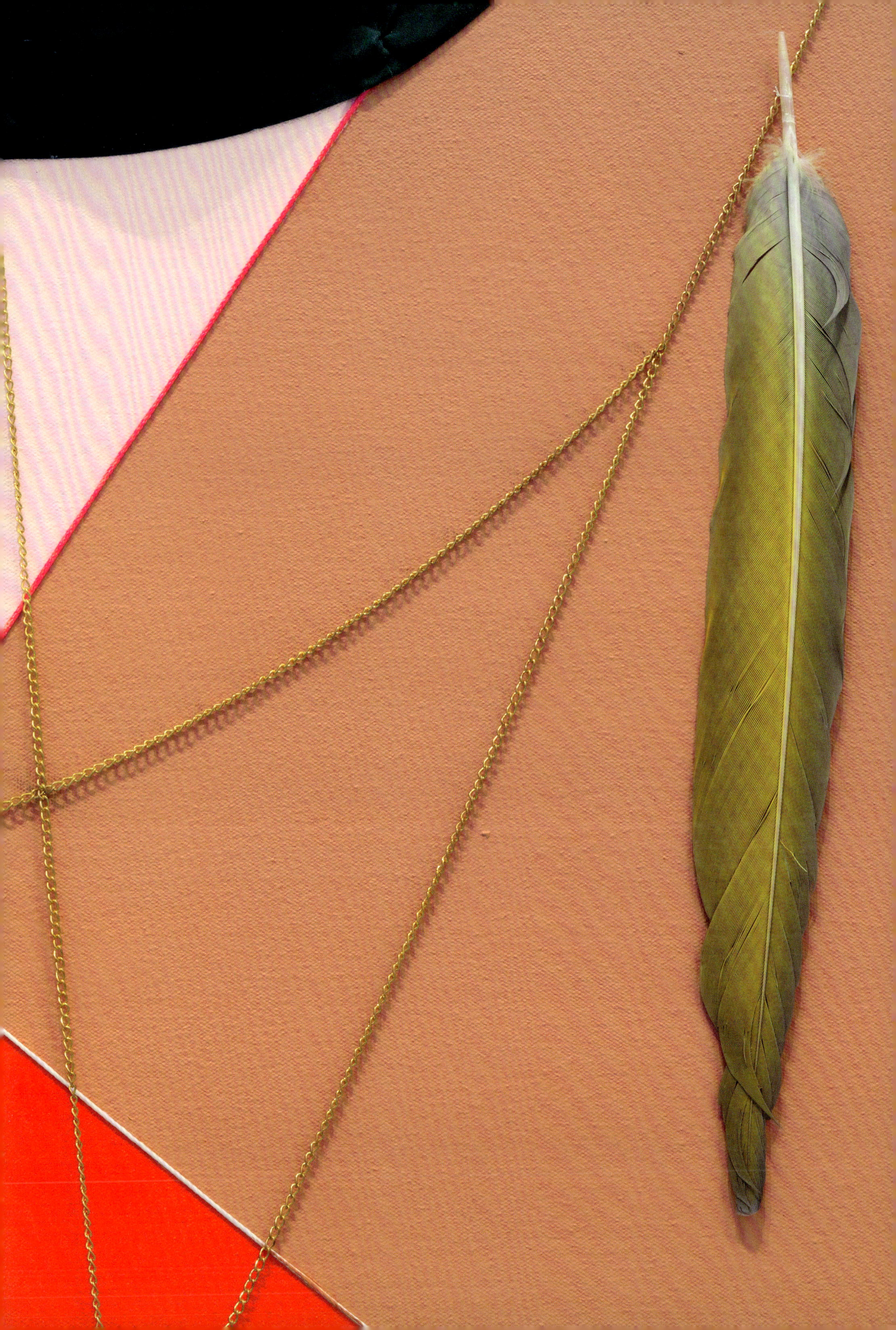

32

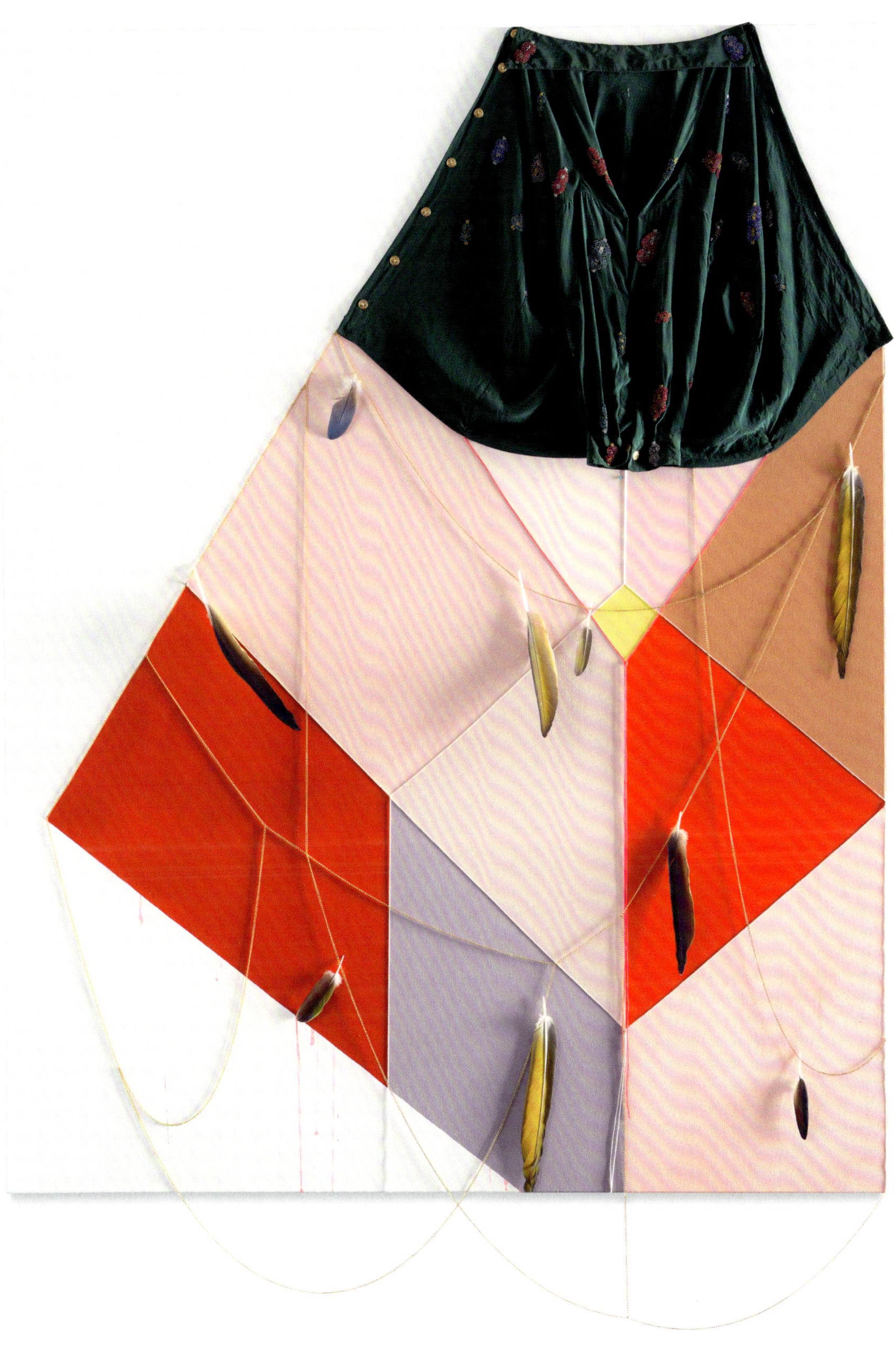

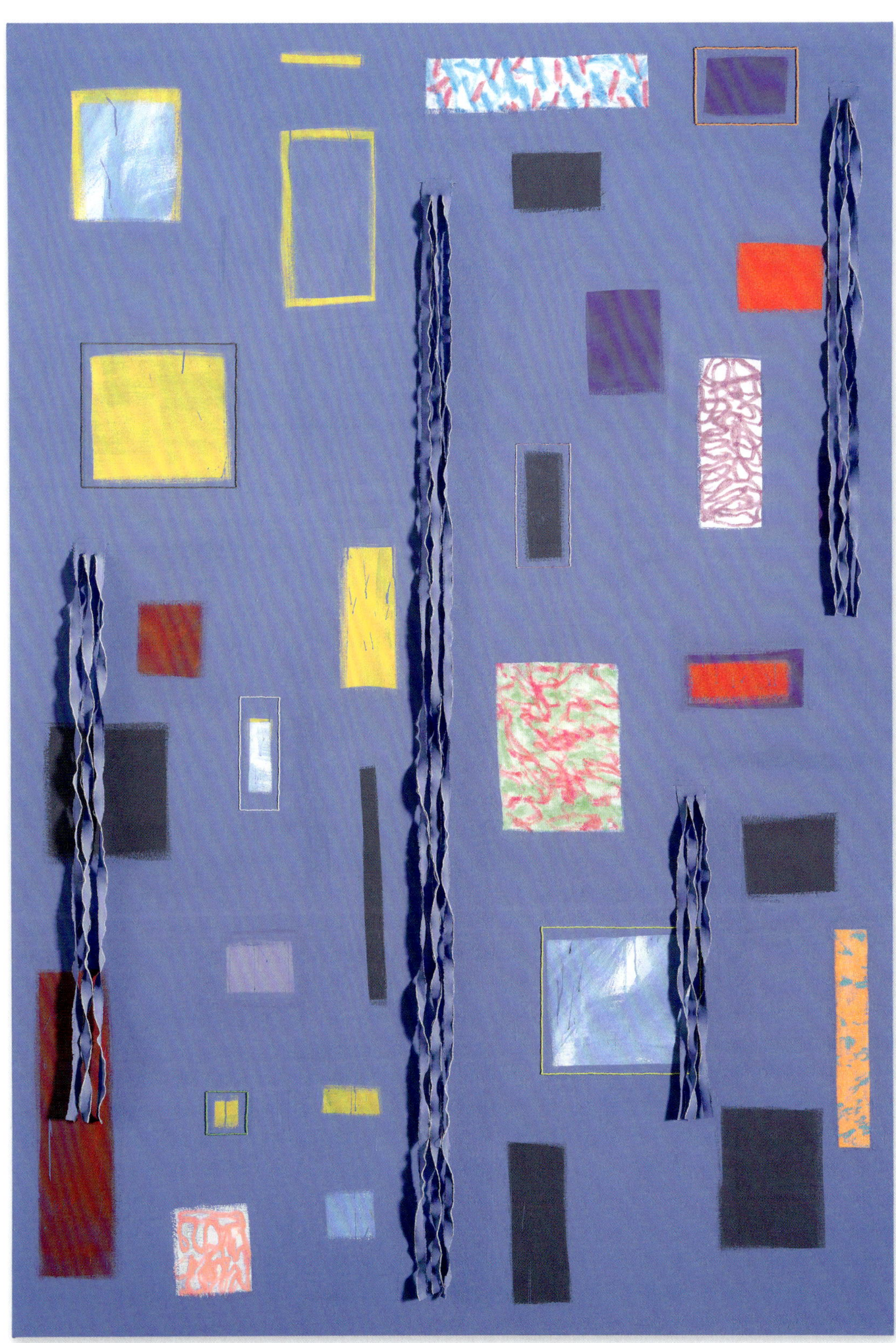

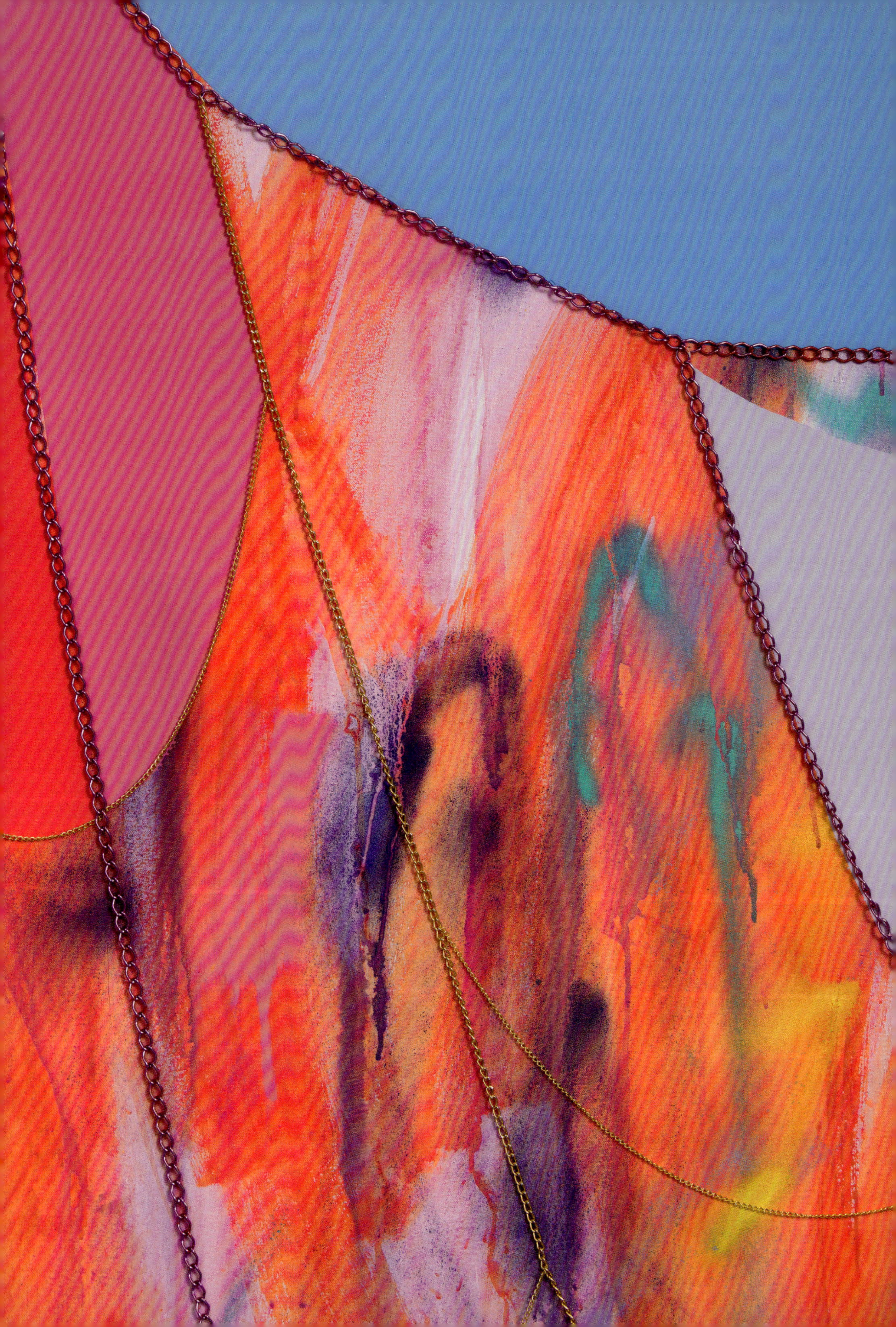

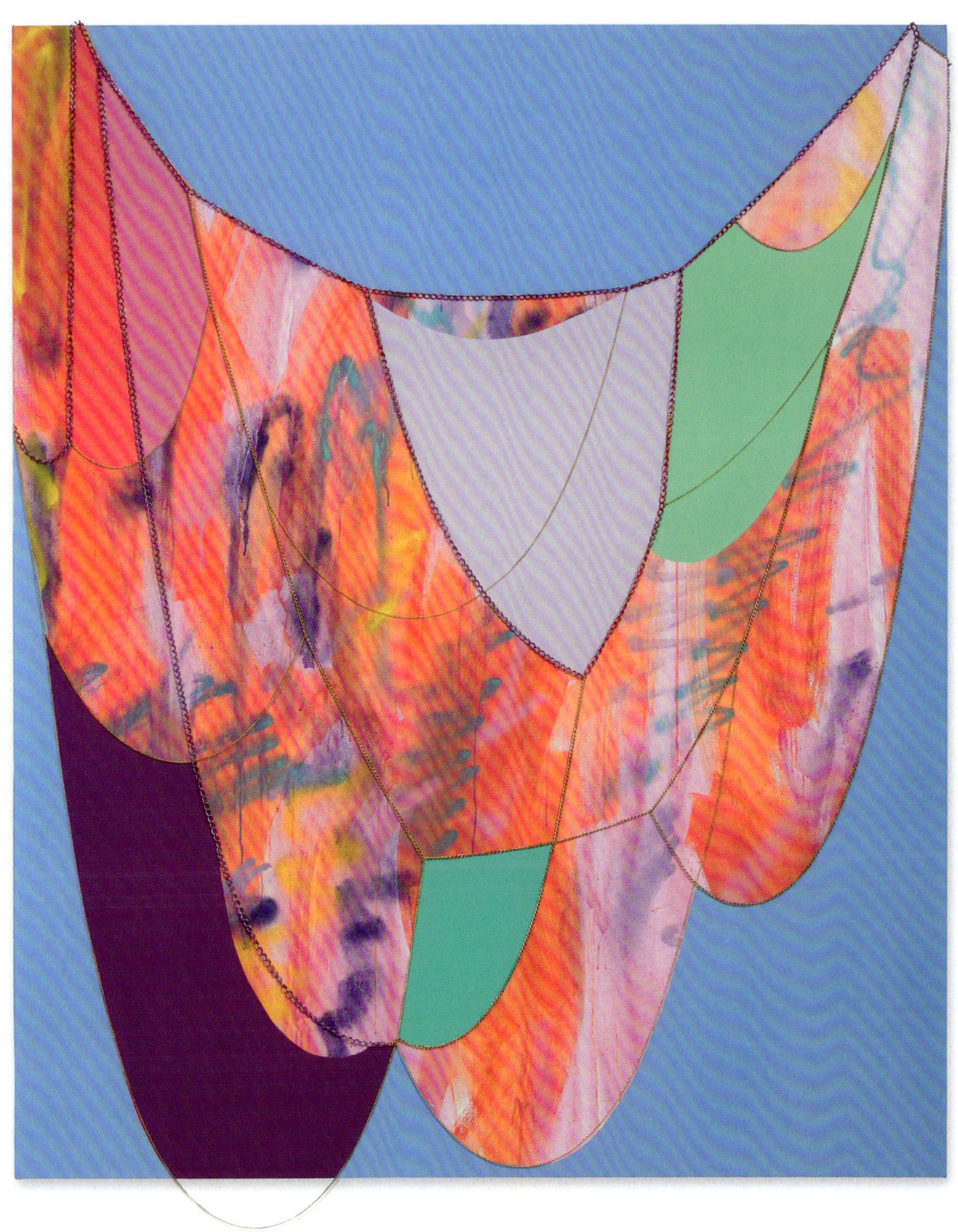

Emotions, 2018

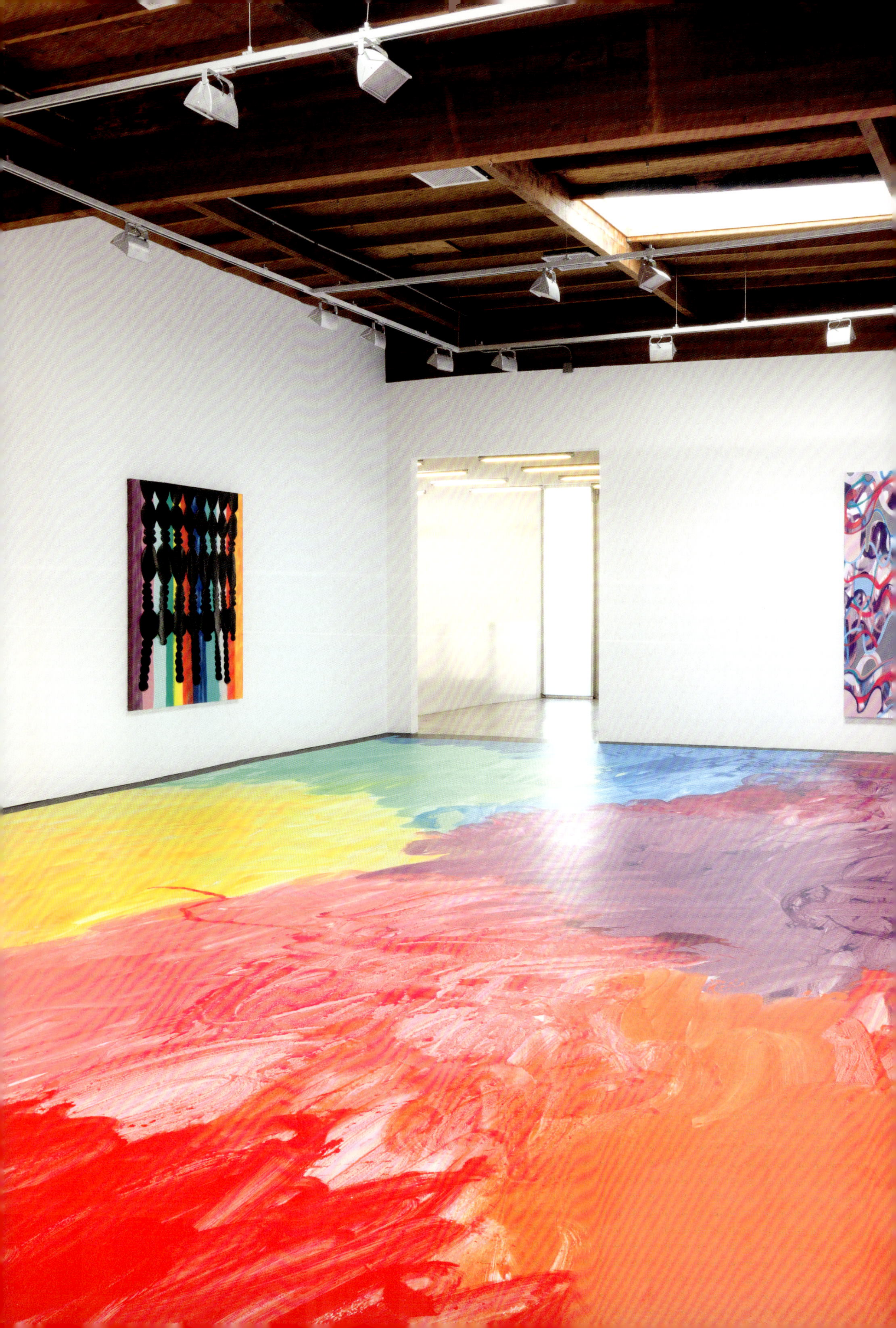

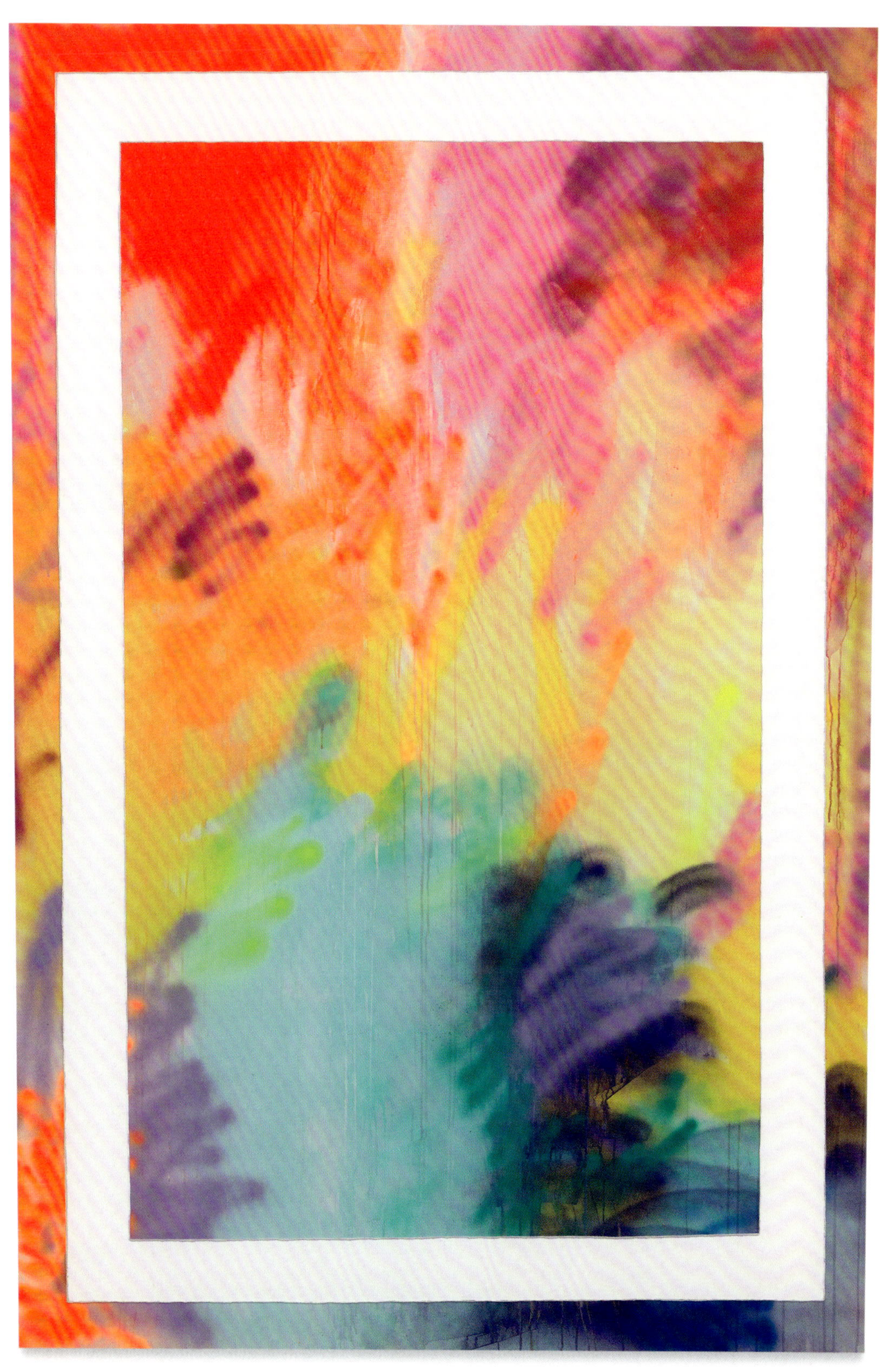

R-E-S-P-E-C-T, 2018

facing, **The Sun Will Not Wait**, Honor Fraser, Los Angeles, 2019

following spread, **Enter the Center**, Tang Teaching Museum at Skidmore College,
Saratoga Springs, New York, 2021

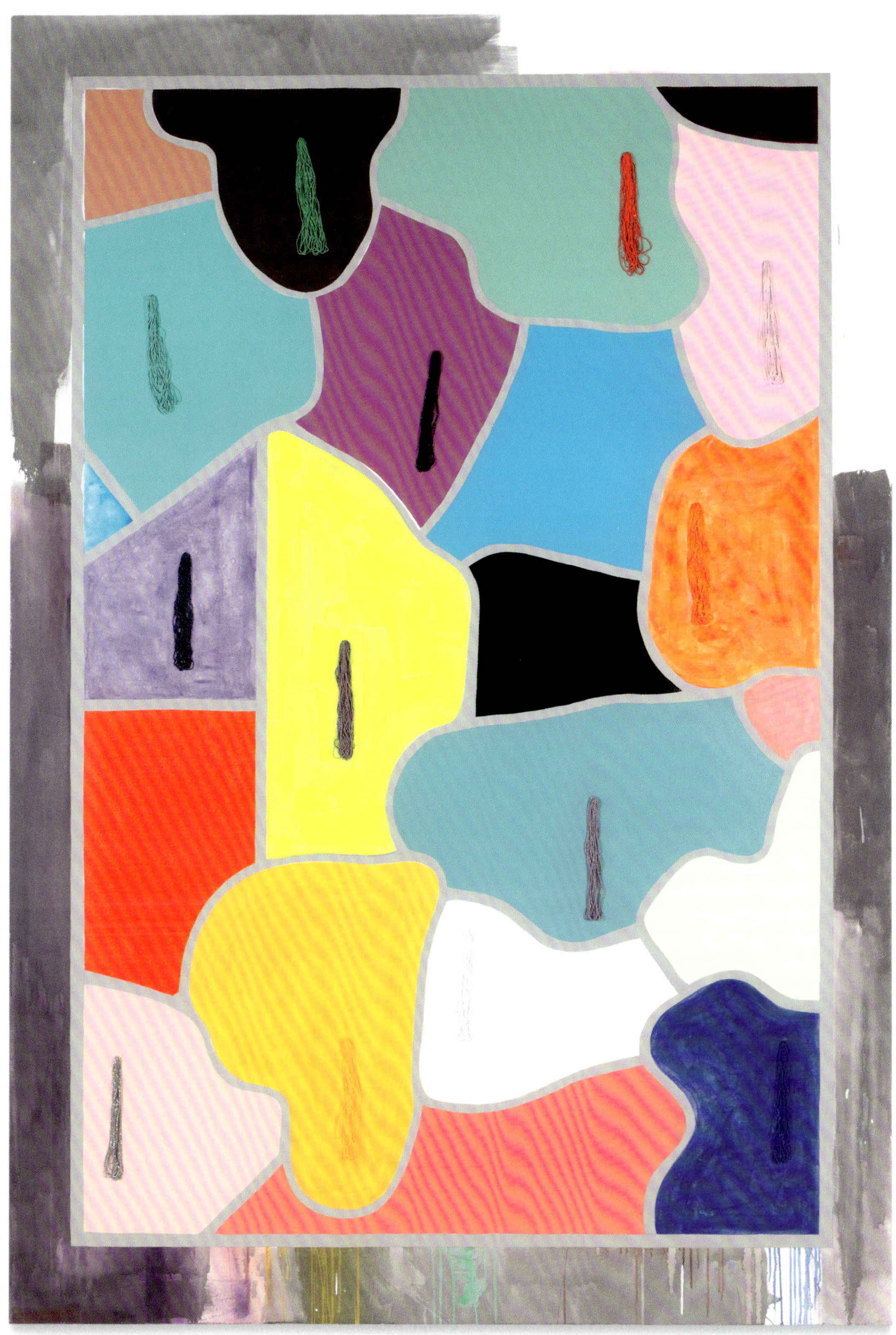

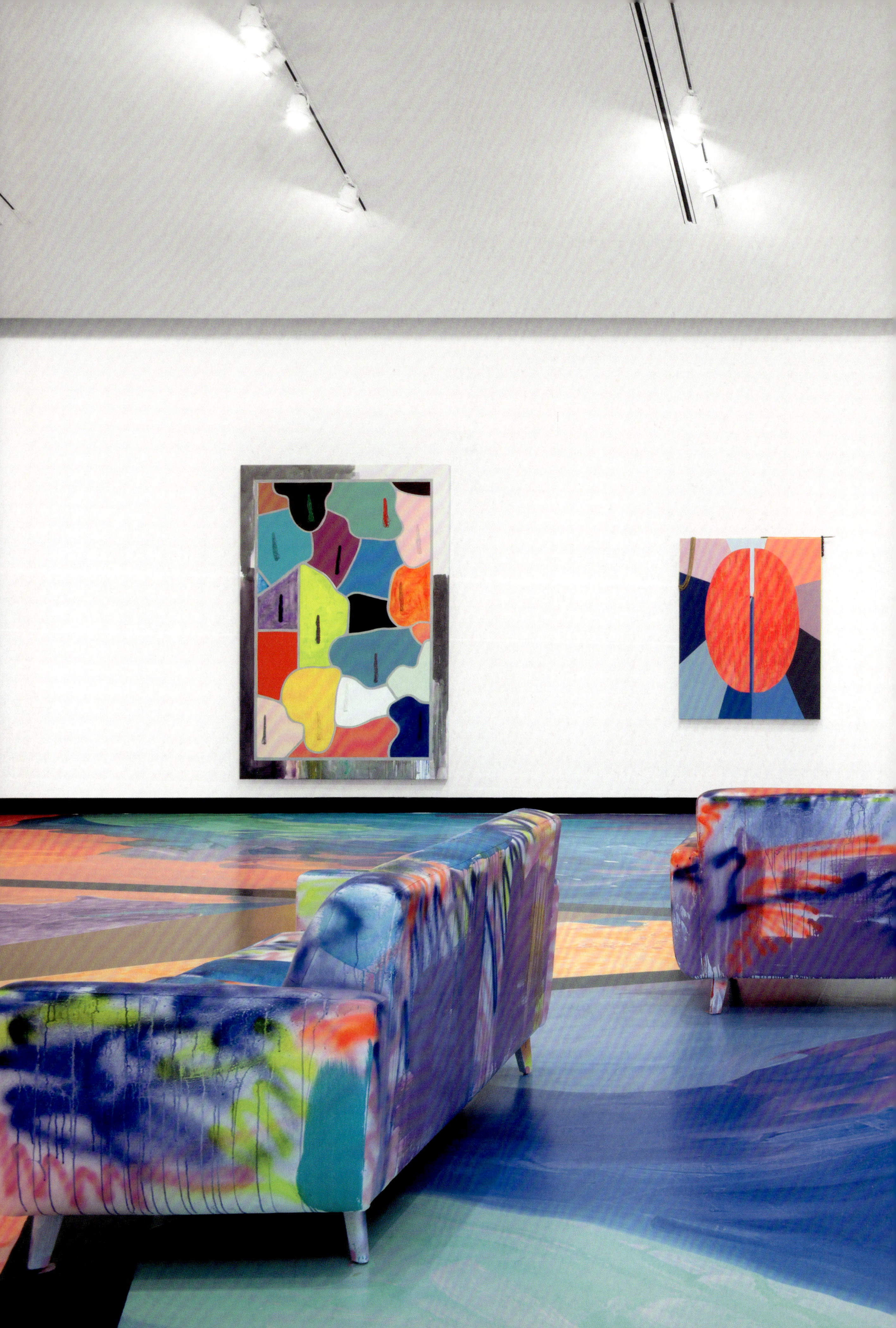

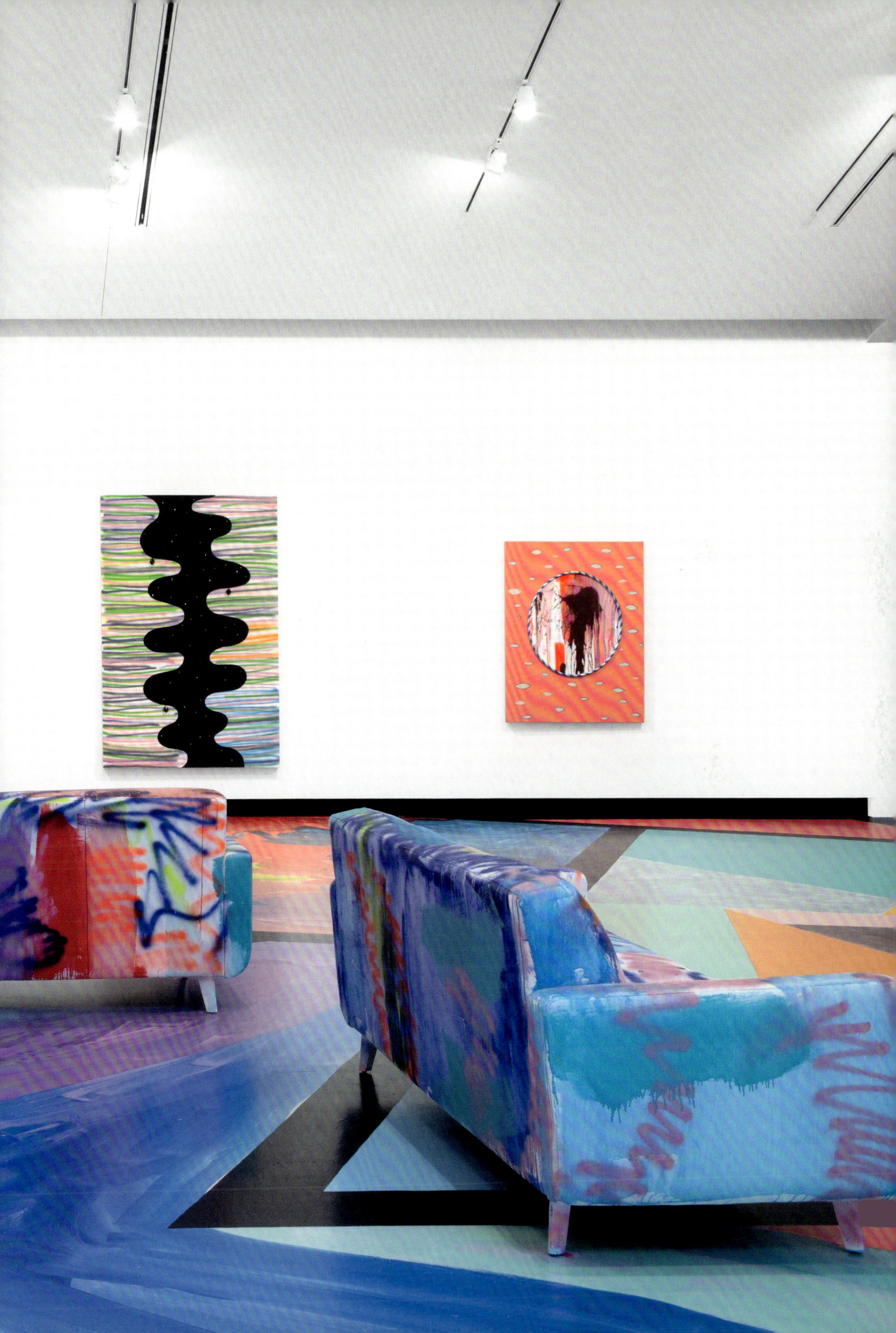

SEE YOU ON MY TERMS

A Dialogue with
Sarah Cain by Ian Berry

IAN BERRY: You grew up in Upstate New York. How did that inform you as an artist?

SARAH CAIN: I think my relationship to space and nature was formed here. And, my desire for solitude—loving to be alone. You have to be able to be alone to be a painter and if you grew up here pre-cell phones, you know how to be alone, which is a very rare thing now.

That's true. I can see how that's a skill you learned from being here.

I like challenge. I like growing. I hate when someone paints the same thing over and over again just to have an iconic thing that means market value. It's so annoying and boring.

But, if you choose the challenge, you choose the risk, and that means you're sometimes going to be lonely.

Maybe, but I think loneliness depends on the person. I don't really get lonely. I'm not really a painter, I'm not really a sculptor. I like the in-between.

You are a painter.

OK. I am a painter.

You're also a contrarian. That's your fuel.

I'm aware of it. Sometimes I wish I could tone it down, but I really can't, and I think that's probably the force it took for me to get out of here. It makes me, it makes the art. I'm fine with it.

I dropped out of high school in 10th grade and left home when I was fifteen. That determination and creative problem solving carries over to my work.

Is that when you went abroad?

Yeah, I left public high school at fifteen to go on a foreign exchange program to the South of France. Then, I went to a junior college in Albany, New York and won a scholarship back to Paris for a year of art school there. I transferred into the San Francisco Art Institute in 1997 and I've been a Californian ever since.

I wonder about the experiences you had and artwork you made as a teenager and how they were formative. When I see pictures of your environmental works from that time, I can piece them together to create a narrative about you as an artist now. When you were rebelling against school, doing your own thing, figuring out your chosen family, and your friends—how was art-making part of all that?

It was always a part of it. I sent a photo of my painting the sofas here at the Tang to my childhood friend who used to paint with me in my parents' basement. I painted the walls and a few sofas there.

As a teenager?

Yeah, as a teenager. I was painting on the walls in the basement of the brand-new house my parents worked so hard to build.

In punk rock tradition.

Yeah, but also totally unaware of that tradition. It wasn't until I was in a high school in France that I met someone who introduced me to Bikini Kill and all of that.

So, you were creating a way to be yourself?

I was figuring out how to get out. I had a couple of key older people that presented examples of a way forward.

Tell me about the East Nassau building and the people who were there in the 90s. What did you make there? Did you live there too?

It was amazing. Martha Lloyd was a painter transplant from Boston. I loved her so much. She and her husband let me live and work in their 8,000 sq ft WPA schoolhouse off and on for over a decade. I had never seen an artist's studio before hers. She had a whole room that was full of poetry books, a garden of night blooming flowers, and also a tea and herb garden. She existed in her own dimension. She made huge paintings. It was a very unlikely friendship with, like, fifty years between us. She let my friends stay there too.

It was an incredibly formative moment. I remember things emotionally through architectural space and the space of that giant school building imprinted on me early on. The poets Bernadette Mayer and Phil Good were their neighbors. Bernadette has been a big presence in my life and the source of many titles for my art for twenty years.

What prompted you to paint the walls and floor of the schoolhouse? Were those meant for you alone?

That was just my figuring out how to be an artist, how to paint. I was so baffled by the financial side of everything. Growing up here, you're usually pretty broke. Moving to San Francisco during the first dot com boom was insane. I was very against making objects that would just end up in a museum. It felt like death to me.

I wanted to make art that was in the present tense, that considered the environment and yet also took on no overhead. That's why I found abandoned buildings. At that time, I limited everything I owned to three suitcases. I would work temporary jobs and then float around. In addition to works I made on-site in the East Nassau building, I did some in Chatham, New York and some in San Francisco too.

Did you think people would see them? Did you want people to see them?

A few people saw them but mostly I knew they would live on in documentation. I painted some in artist-run spaces in San Francisco that more people saw. That's actually how my career started—from there, I met art world people.

How did you connect and build a network?

I curated shows in my house with friends that people would come to, but the real break was from Tara McDowell, who was a curator at San Francisco MoMA. The first time I was up for the SECA Award—an award and show they give to local artists—I took an SF MoMA group through an abandoned building in San Francisco, where I made five or six works.

I had done a show at the artist-run space Queen's Nails Annex in San Francisco and I ran into Tara who was working on a Richard Tuttle retrospective. He's one of my favorites. She said, "Oh, I'll bring him by to see your show." Richard Tuttle was having dinner with Tony Meier so he came too. I had wanted to show at Tony's gallery, and that's how it started. Tony gave me a show.

That was your first gallery show?

Yes. Then I set up again for SF MoMA at Tony's gallery and that time they gave me the SECA award. So, I had my first museum show and first gallery show in 2006.

When you're making these paintings on-site, you don't have a sketchbook, and you don't draw them out. You don't project images and you don't get up on a ladder to look. Did you always work that way?

Yeah. I do a lot of looking but usually not from a ladder. I work fast.

I assume there were moments you learned what you could do, so that you are now able to walk into a big room with a finite amount of time, and confidently say, "Yeah, I can do this."

It's kind of crazy the way I work. I see it. I just see everything. I am receptive to these flashes of what to do next. But, I have to be in the right mindset to see it. I'm understanding it more and learning not to freak out. I'm learning to direct a little bit more with assistants. I just believe in it. I don't doubt it. There's nothing else I'm on this earth for in the same way.

Do you like to think of your installations as site-specific, site-responsive?

I'd say they're site-specific paintings. They're definitely not murals, that drives me fucking crazy.

Maybe they're not really site-responsive. From looking at those early pictures, I used to think that's how you worked.

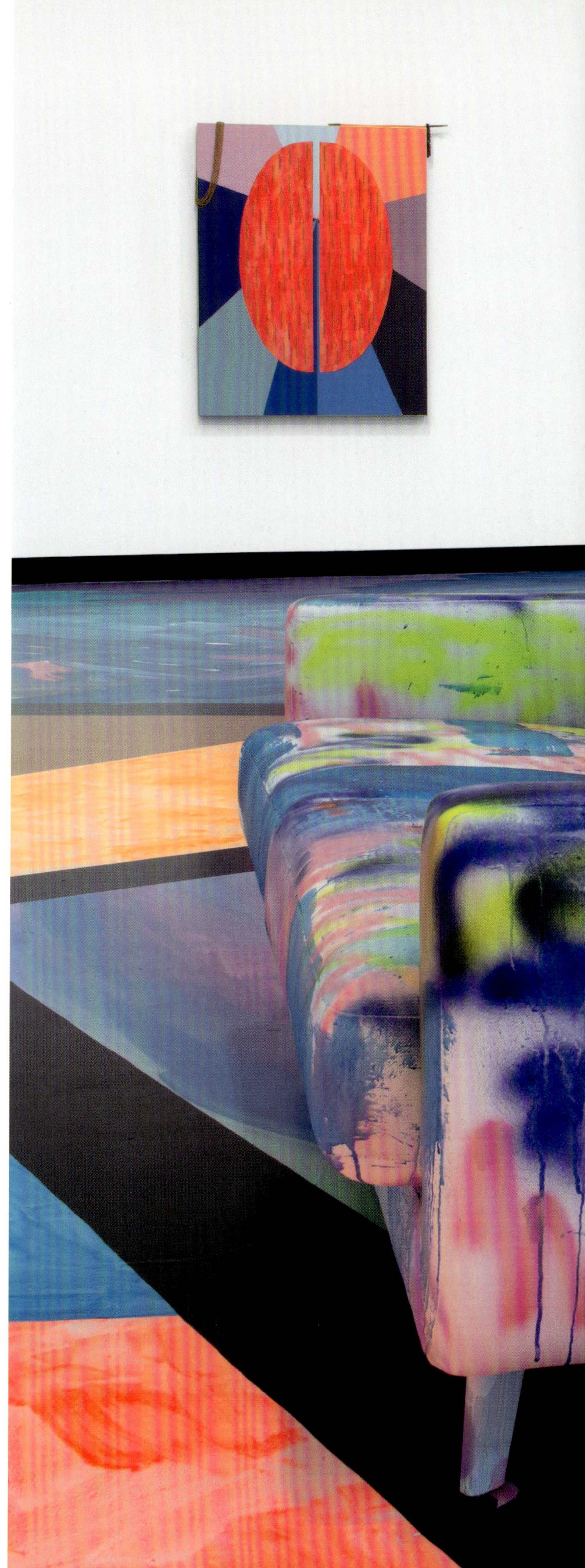

Enter the Center, Tang Teaching Museum at
Skidmore College,
Saratoga Springs, New York, 2021

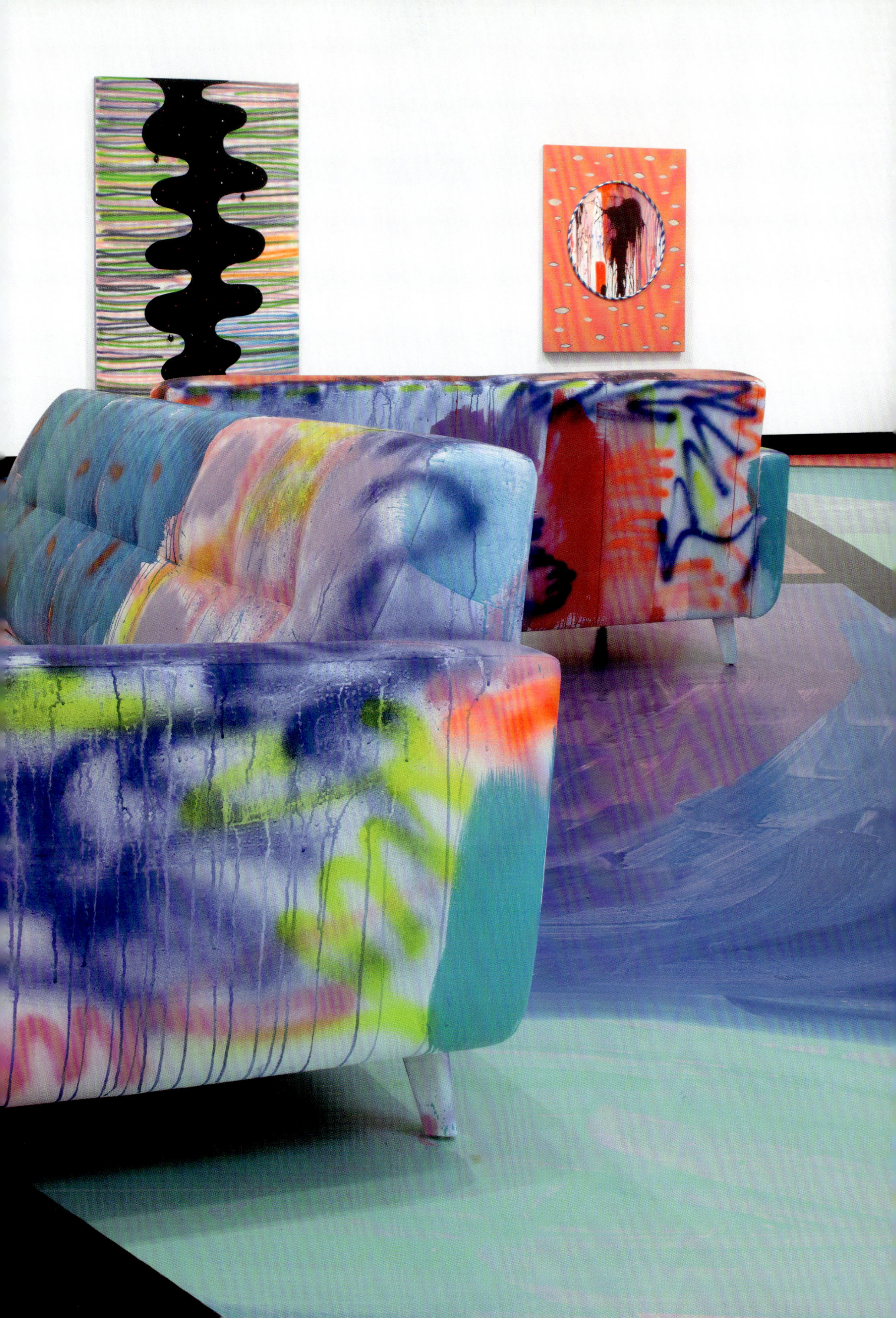

They are responsive energetically and also to the site, but less and less in ways that are easy to pin down. In the beginning, I would sometimes research the space and then maybe they would echo actual shadows and pull in architecture. But, I think over time they have become more energetic portraits of time and space.

Energetic as in the energy of a place or the people there?

Everything, all of it.

So, it's the energy of your experience, your context?

Yeah, but also the world—what's happening during the install, what I'm listening to, and reading, etc. I can feel a lot of things outside of myself; there's an empathetic pulse to the work. There's a section in the Tang floor that seems like an Ian portrait.

No!

It is. Those are your colors. I've done that before. There's a lot of portraiture happening without knowing.

How, as a viewer, can I see that in one of your paintings?

I don't know if that's important. I wrestle with personal narrative. I've made paintings that are so sad, and then a stranger will write to me and say, "I saw this painting and I sat down and cried." If you're an emotionally open person, you feel it. You don't know the details of what happened, but some people feel it. There's a translation of emotions and moments in time that happen through painting. Sometimes I title them after the people that they are portraits of.

When you make paintings on stretched canvases in your studio, are you in the same headspace as when you are 'attacking' a floor or a wall?

It's not as crazy. The works on-site are made with an intense, hyped-up energy.

Do you paint every day?

Probably. I'm in the studio every day. Sometimes I try to take a day off but I tend to work every day.

Whenever I visit you in your studio, you have multiple paintings in progress at the same time.

I do.

It doesn't look like you're using the same tools or even the same supports, and yet, they're existing in the same eye space. Are you going from one to another? Do you shift gears?

I shift depending on where I am mentally each day, that's what I'll pick up on. Sometimes I put them away and sometimes it's like changing gears on a bike. I'll start here and then work up to something. But, you can't just skip to 10. You have to get there.

You're saying you use the other paintings around to warm up?

The paintings shift where they are over time. They change levels. I read about how Neil Young does calisthenics for 10 minutes right before he's going to play on the "Tonight Show" or something, so he's in the zone when he gets there. I feel like there's a lot of that in the studio. Sometimes even cleaning the studio or reorganizing the brushes is a stage for getting to the first painting that then jumps to the second.

But the second painting is the one that's really cooking?

Maybe the fourth or fifth.

This show at the Tang focuses on works from the last decade.

I think the work shifted in that moment.

I agree. There is something about this group of work that holds together as a moment in your history.

I moved to Los Angeles in 2007. My first show with Honor Fraser was in 2012: it was called *freedom is a prime number*, a line I lifted from a Roberto Bolaño novel. I loved working with Honor. It was a big change at the time. I moved into a bigger studio, finally had local support, a big gallery, an enthusiastic local dealer. I was coming into my own. From that point on, most of the canvases have collaged elements.

Artists can come into their own and not have an opportunity to show their work, which stifles so many painters. If you're living with a decade of your work, it kind of kills your spirit. It's good to get them out into the world. It's weird to be in here at the Tang surrounded by all of these old ones—it's like my life is just looking at me.

Do you want to run away when you walk into the gallery and see all these paintings?

No, I like it. I don't repeat myself, so it's exciting. I remember things that I've done once that I really like. I think because we were working on our show at the same time as my National Gallery show, my installation there, *My favorite season is the fall of the patriarchy,* has a little sampling from a lot of things in here. I like seeing these all together. They make me happy.

This show is really important. It's a good marker. After this, I can let go of whatever teenage runaway drama I have. Done it, came back, see you later. Bye. See you on my terms.

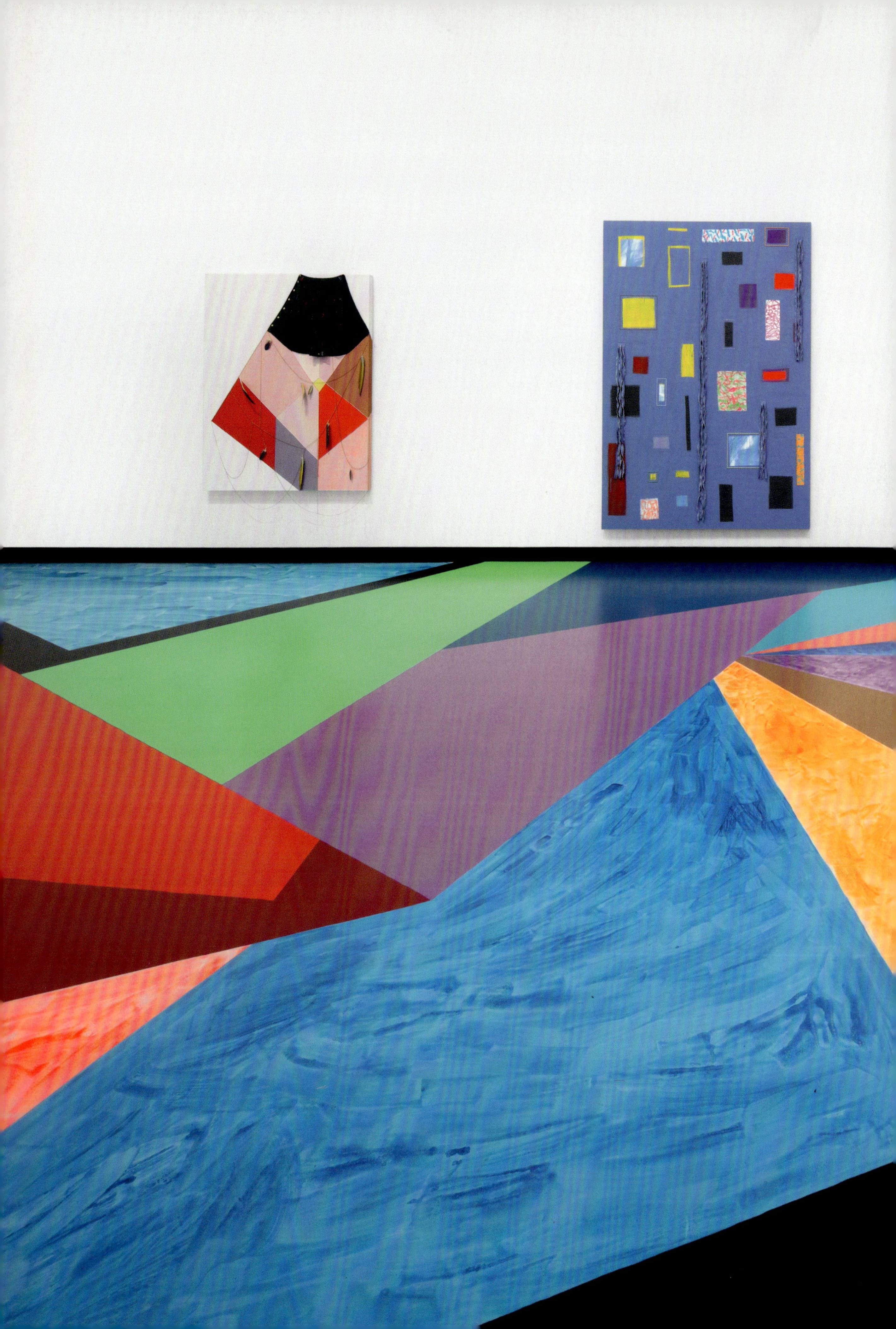

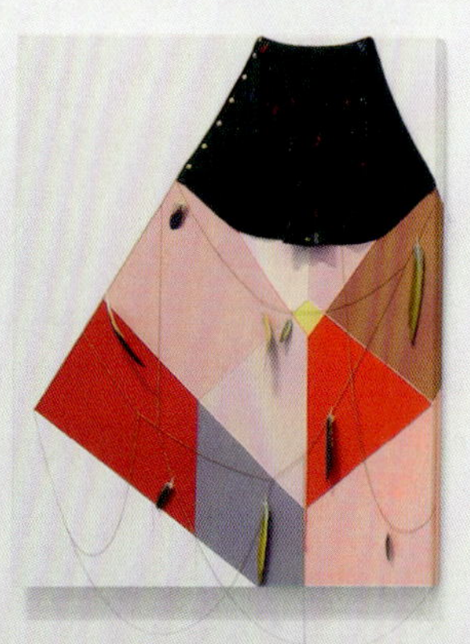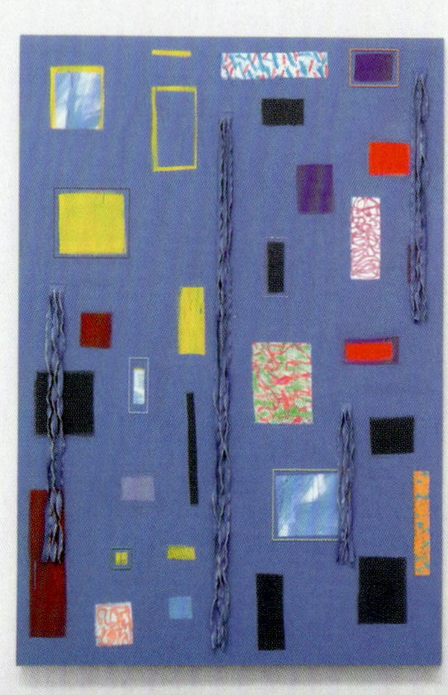

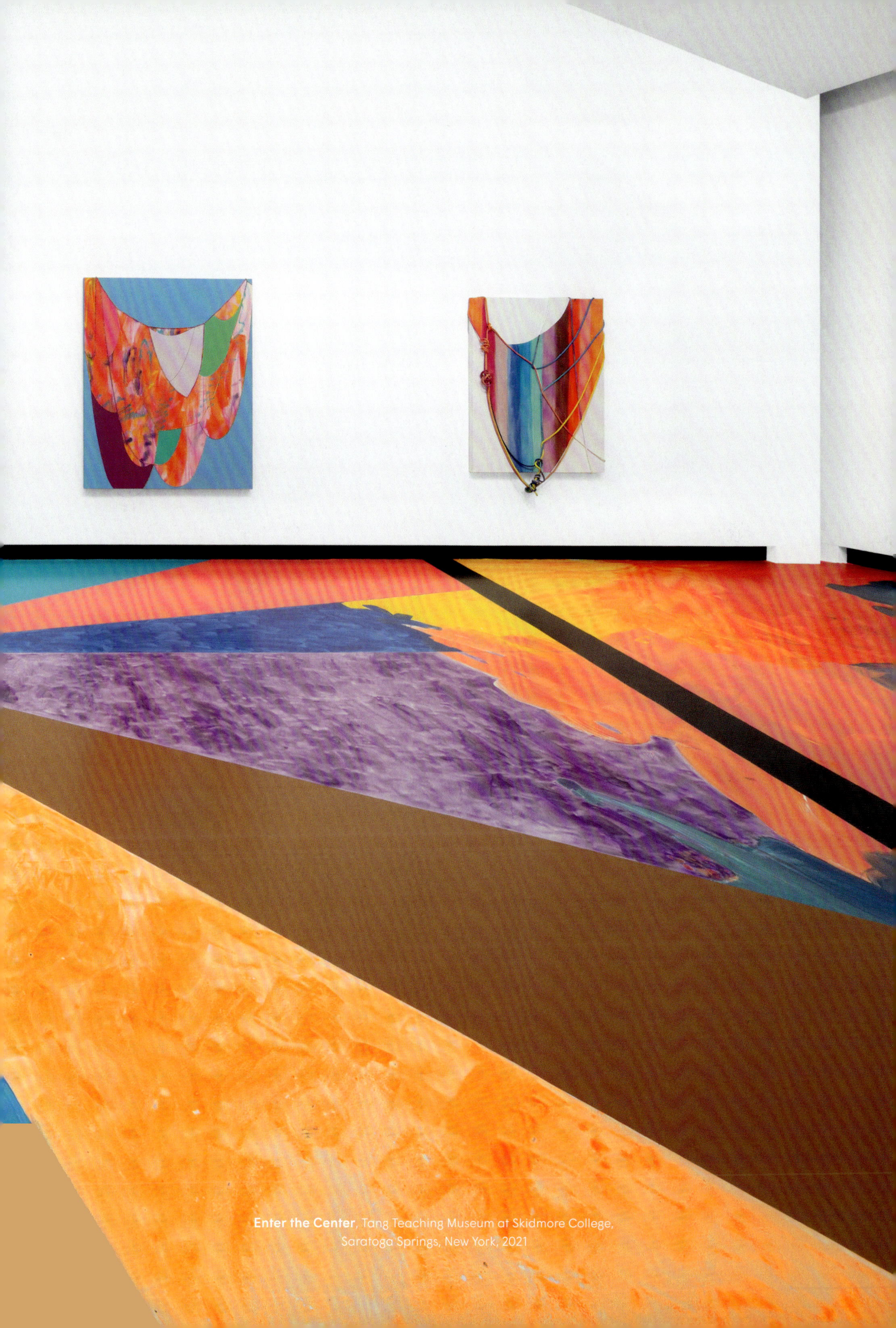

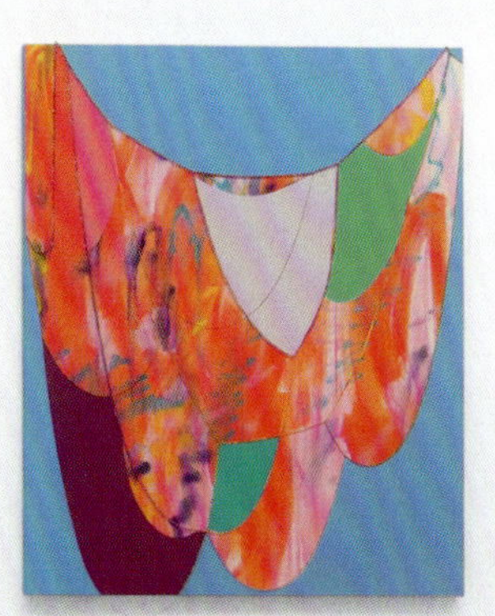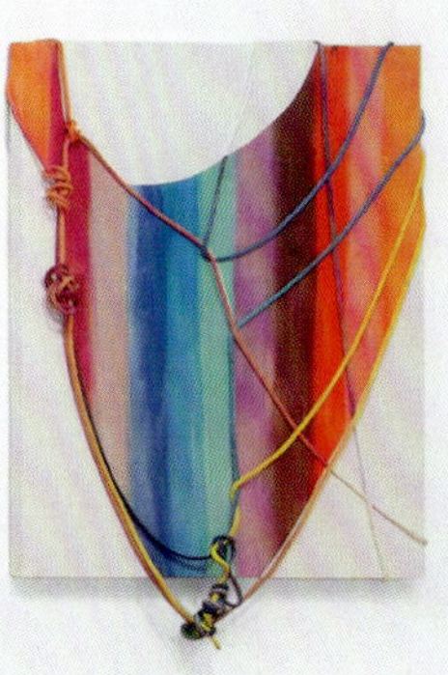

Enter the Center, Tang Teaching Museum at Skidmore College,
Saratoga Springs, New York, 2021

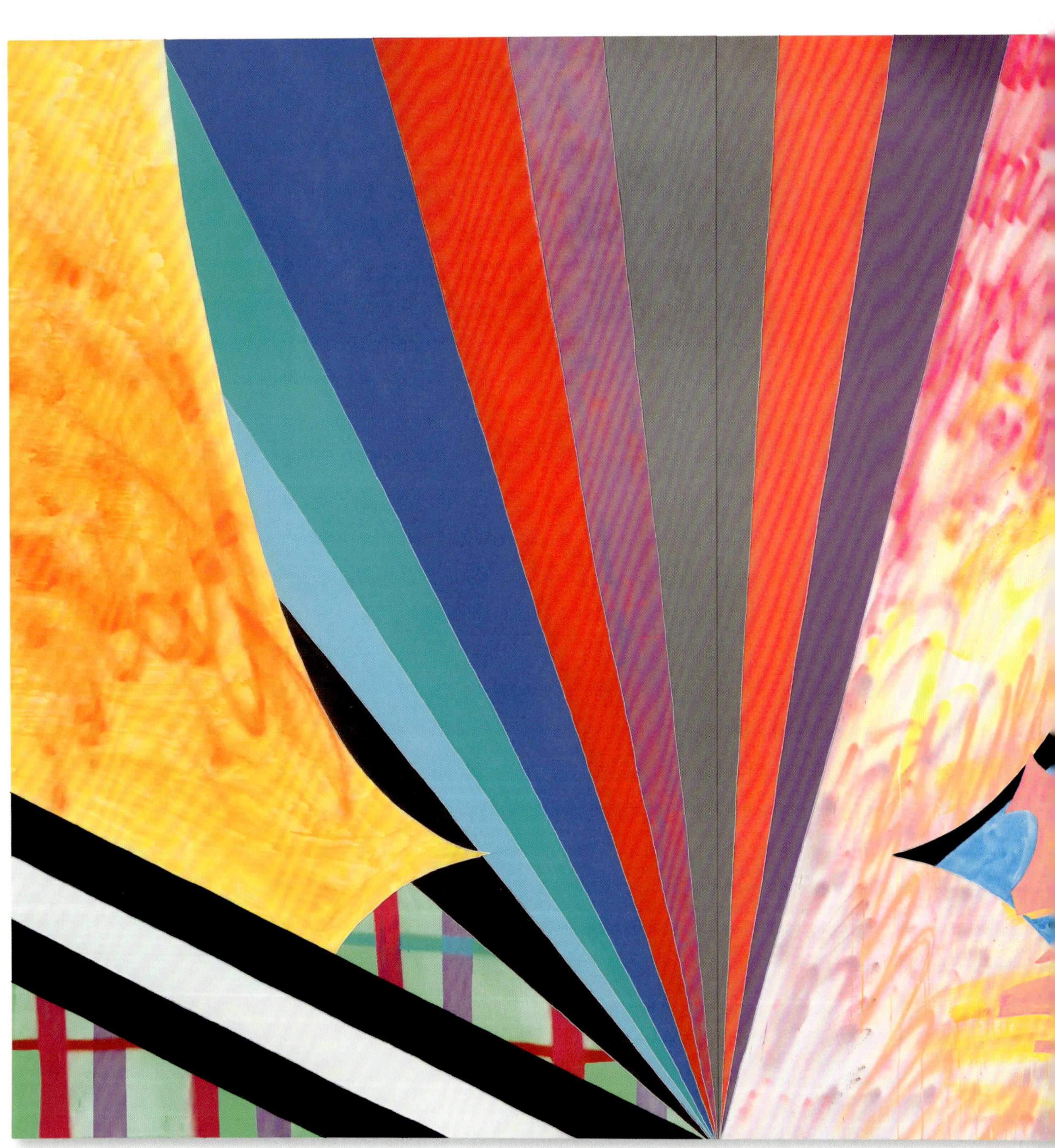

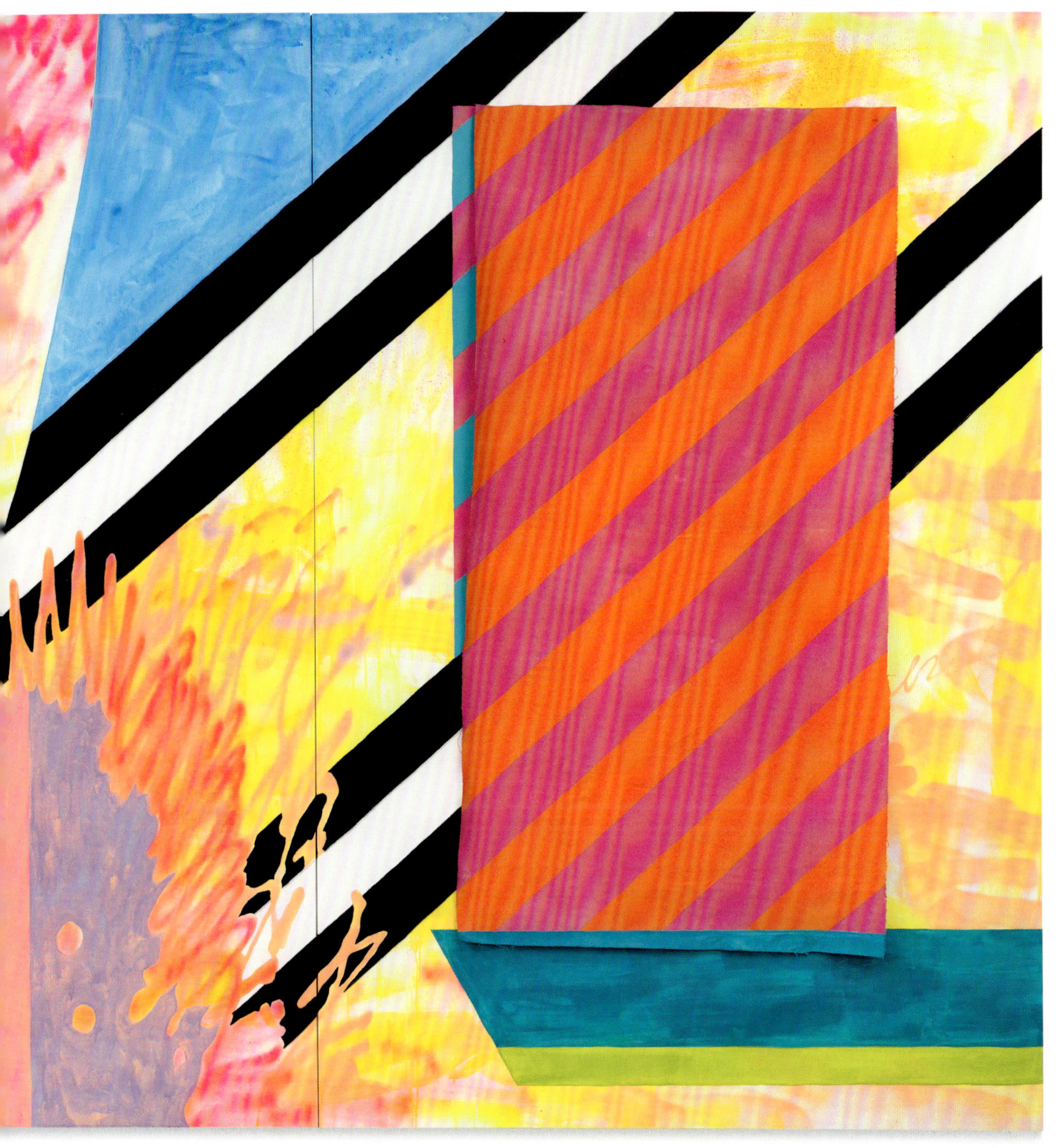

The Era Of, 2021

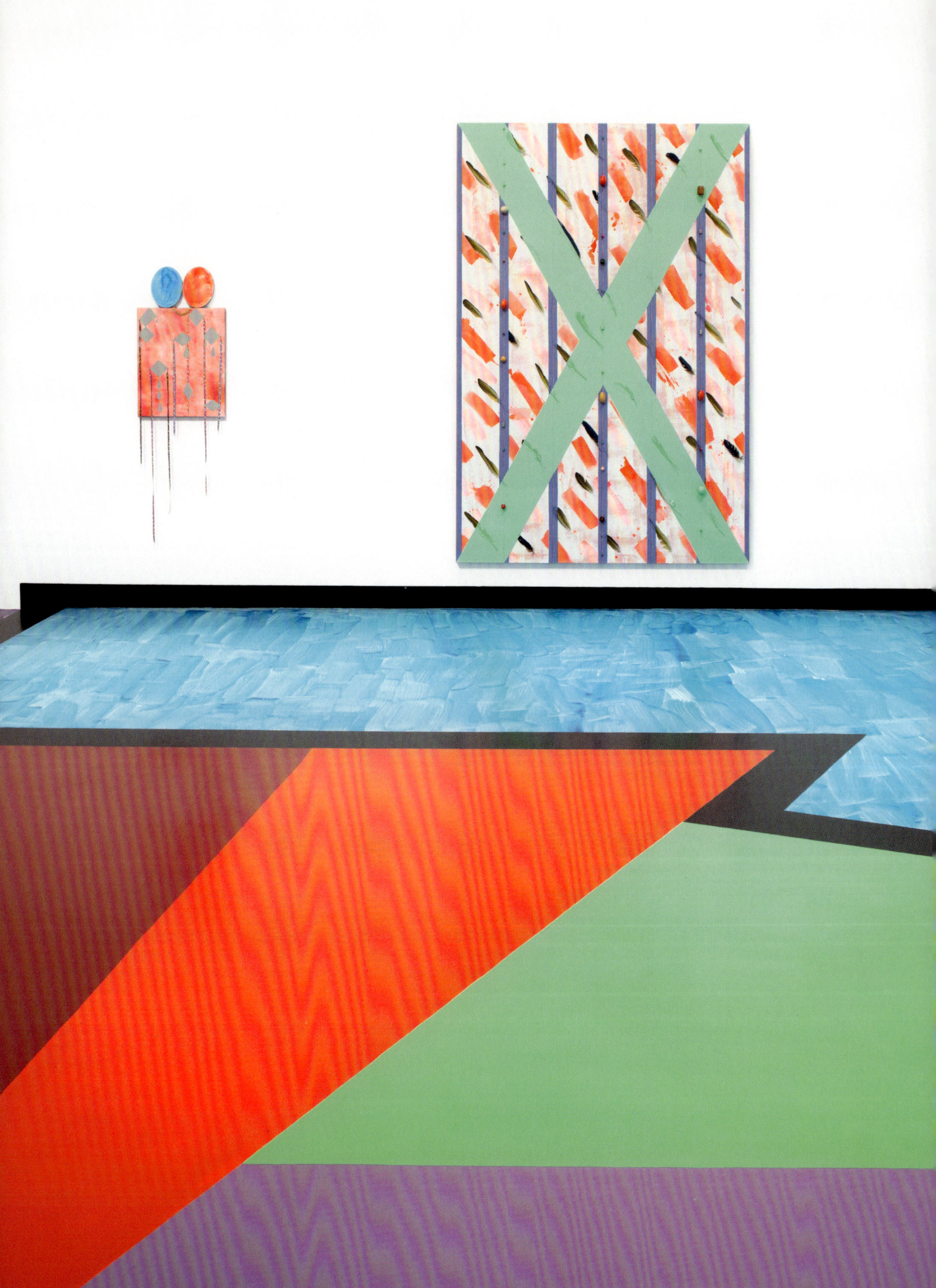

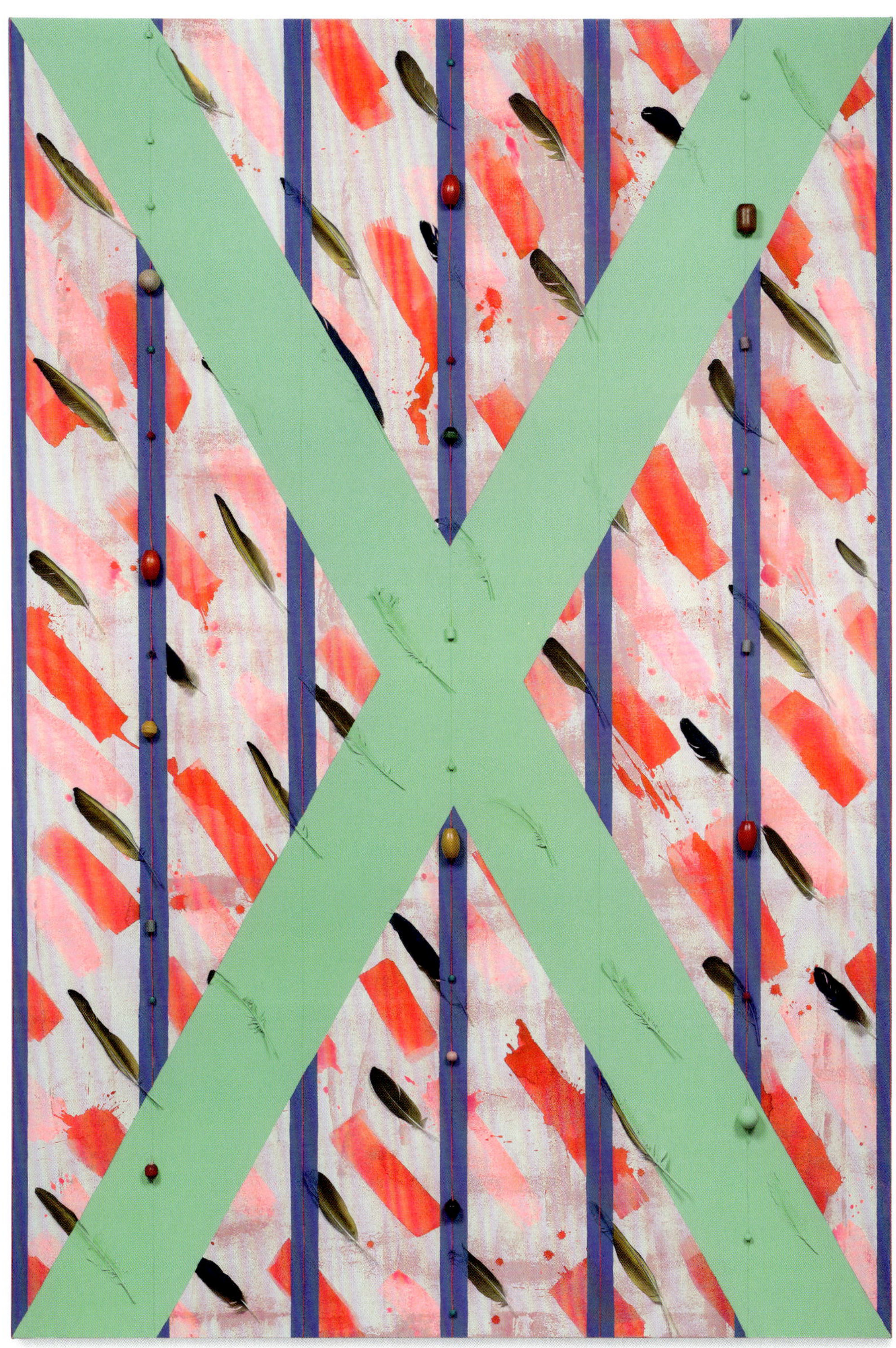

mint green X, 2015

facing, **Enter the Center**, Tang Teaching Museum at Skidmore College,
Saratoga Springs, New York, 2021

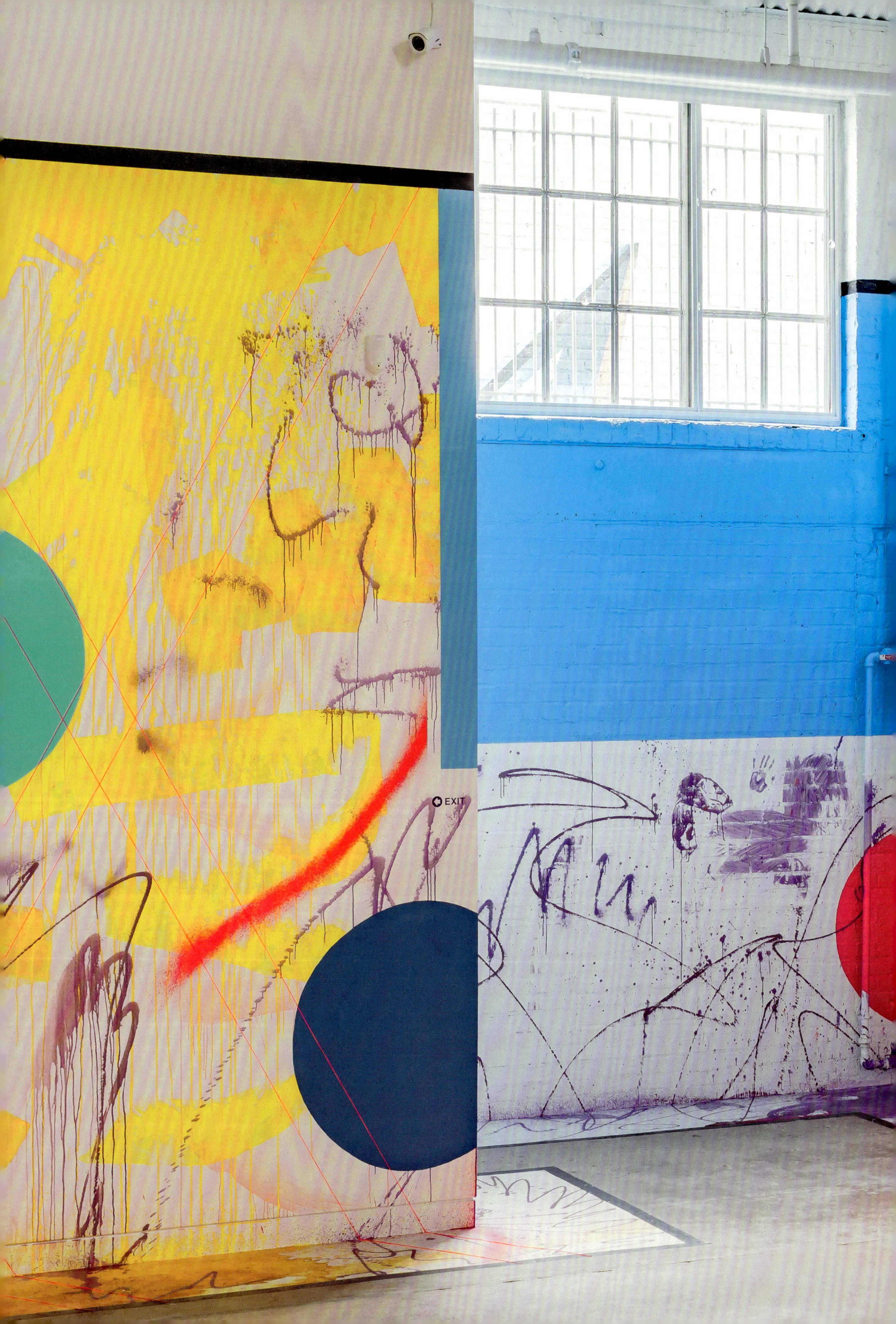

EXIT

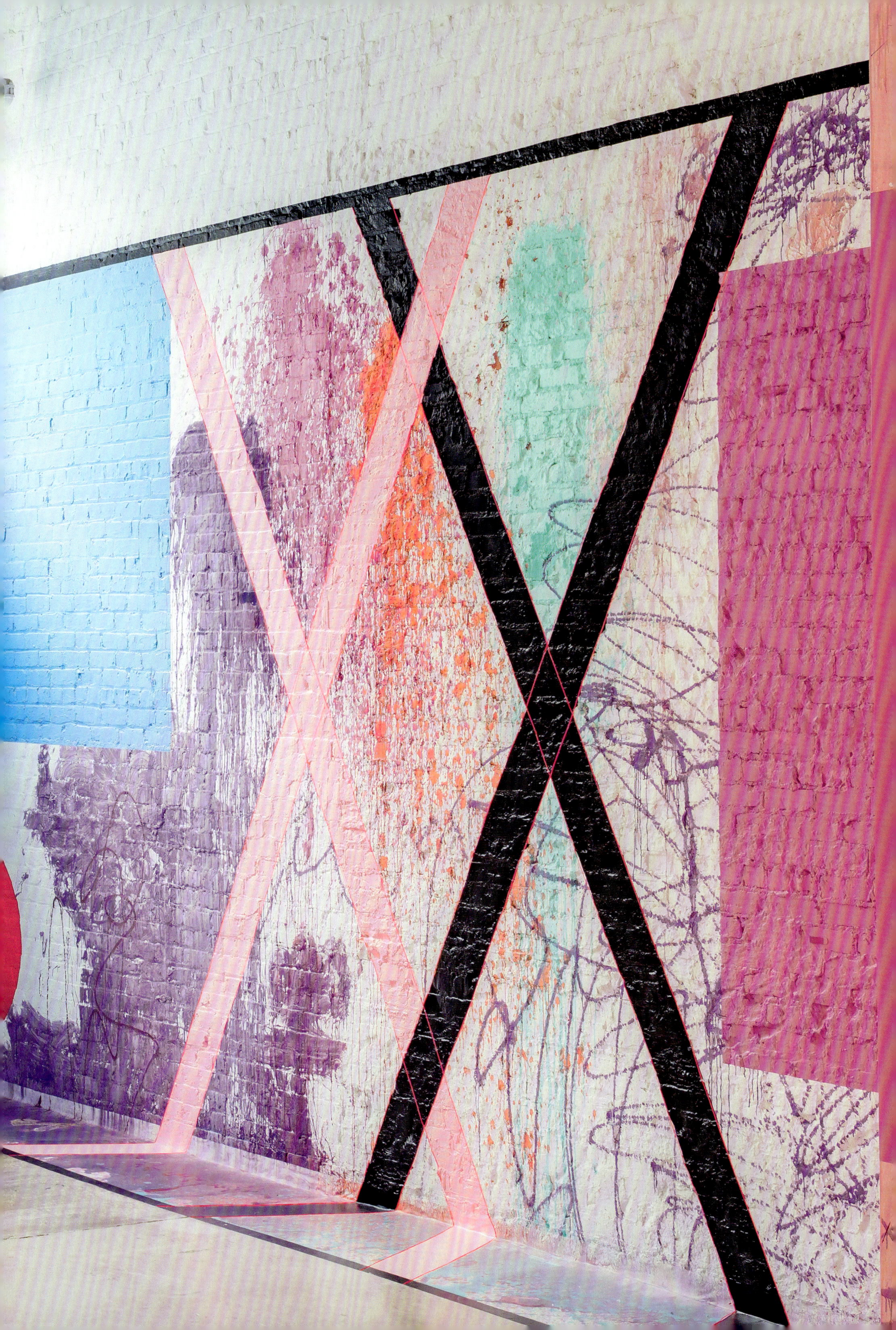

preceding spread, **The Imaginary Architecture of Love**,
Contemporary Art Museum, Raleigh, 2015

love seat, 2015

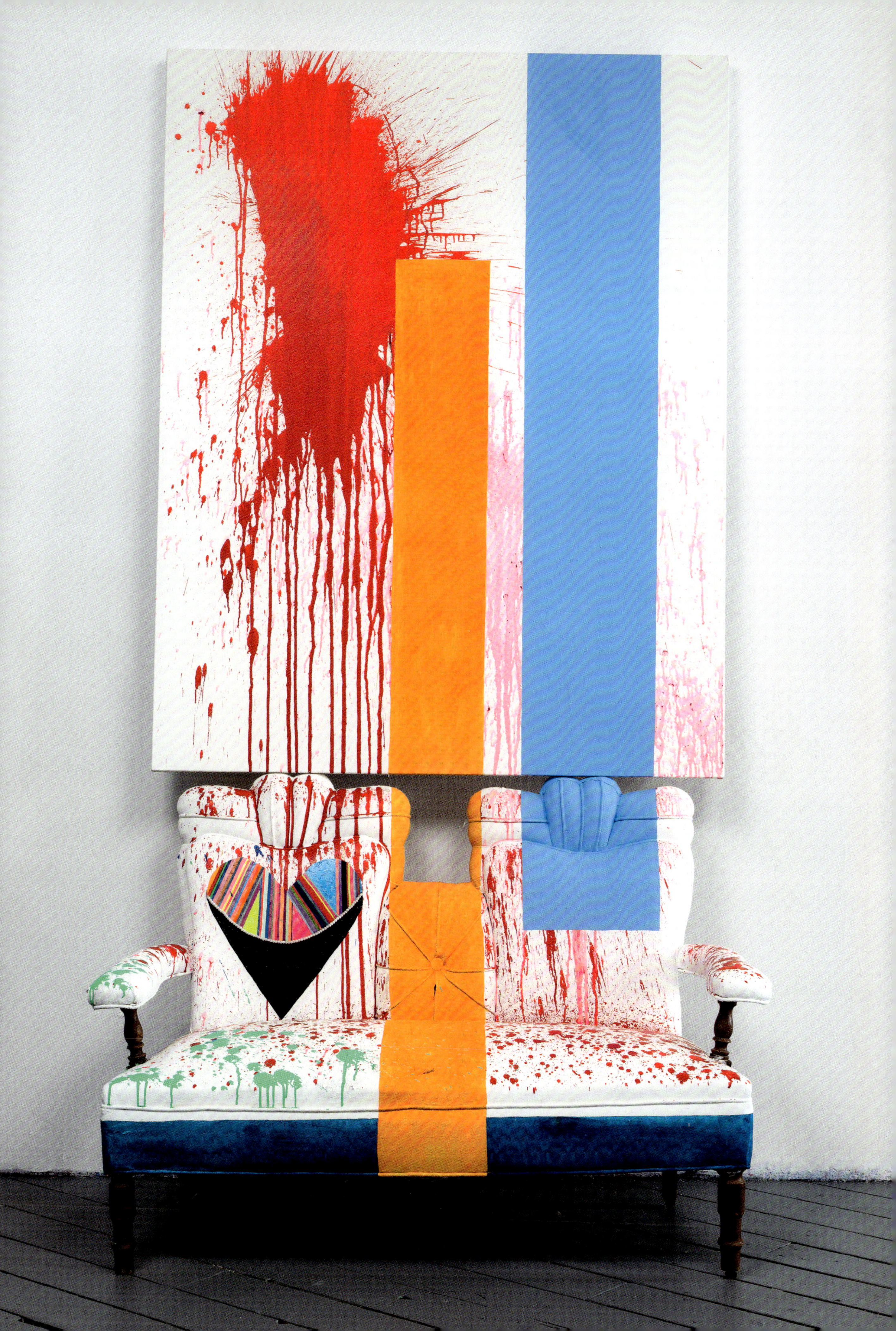

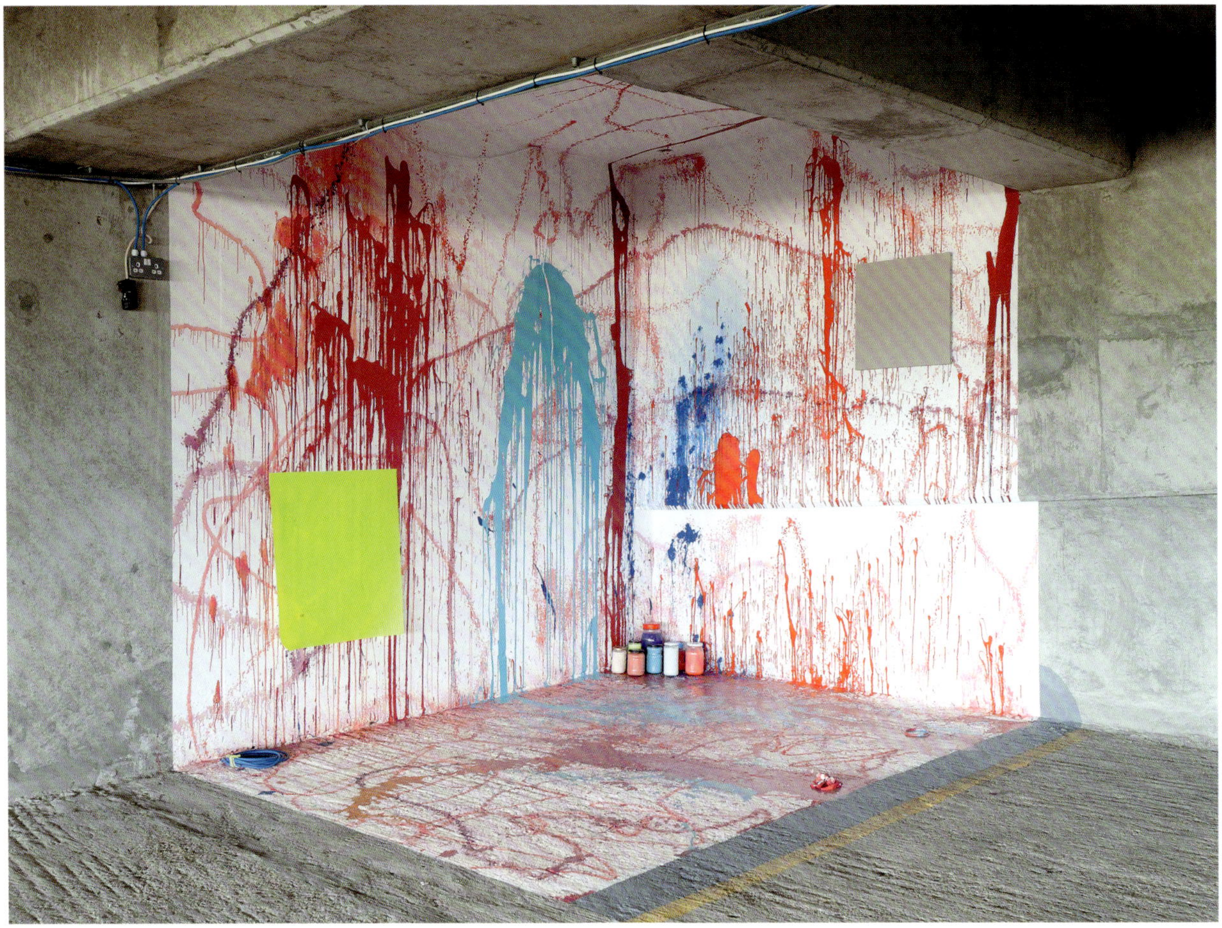

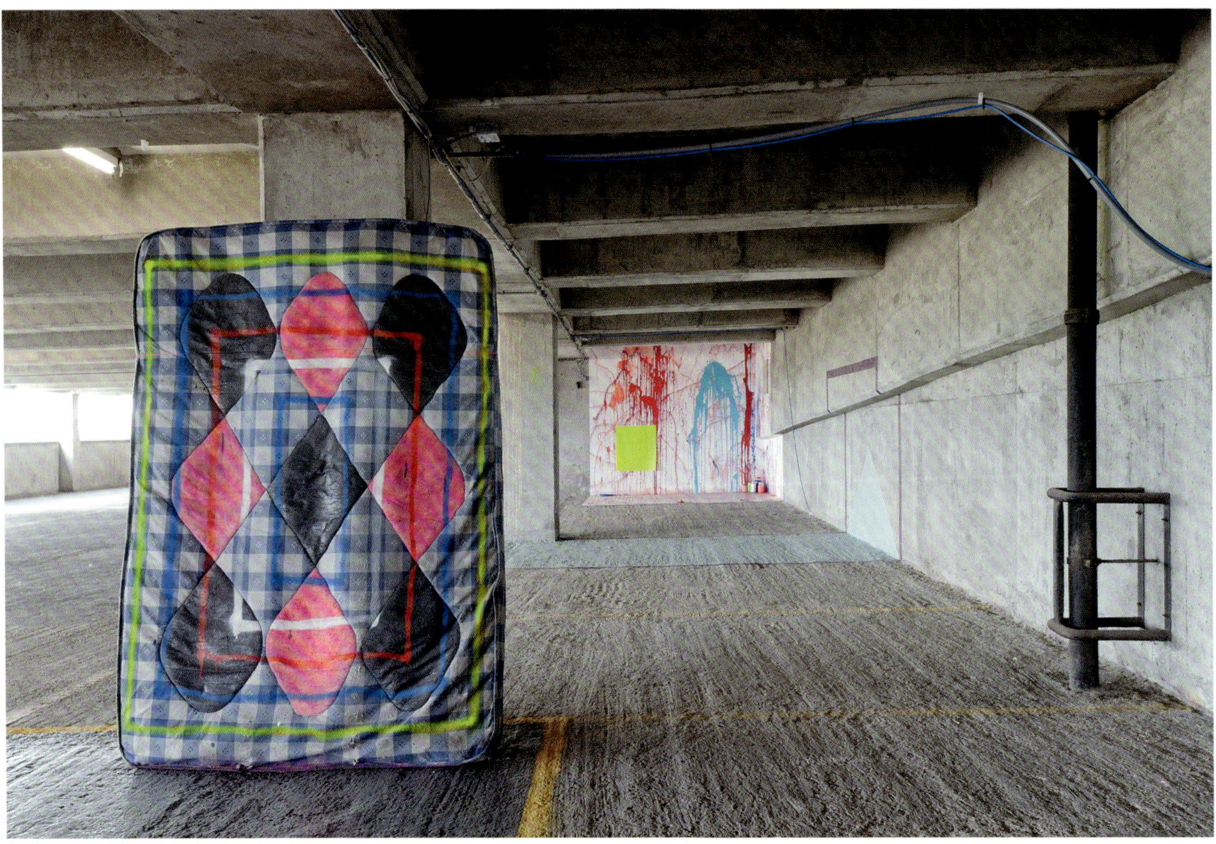

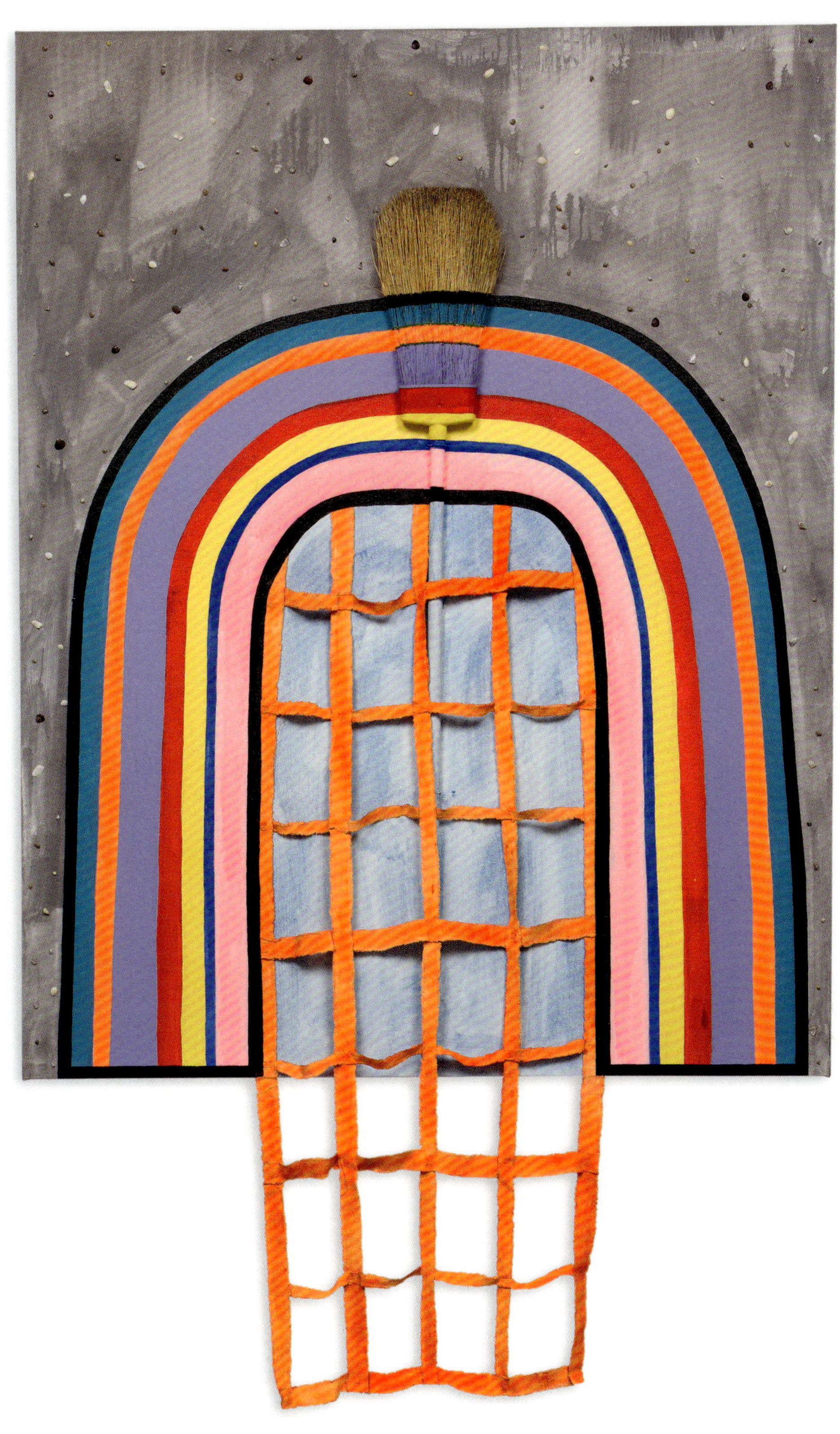

witchcraft, 2015

facing, **AS IF ONLY**, London, 2012

Mister, 2012

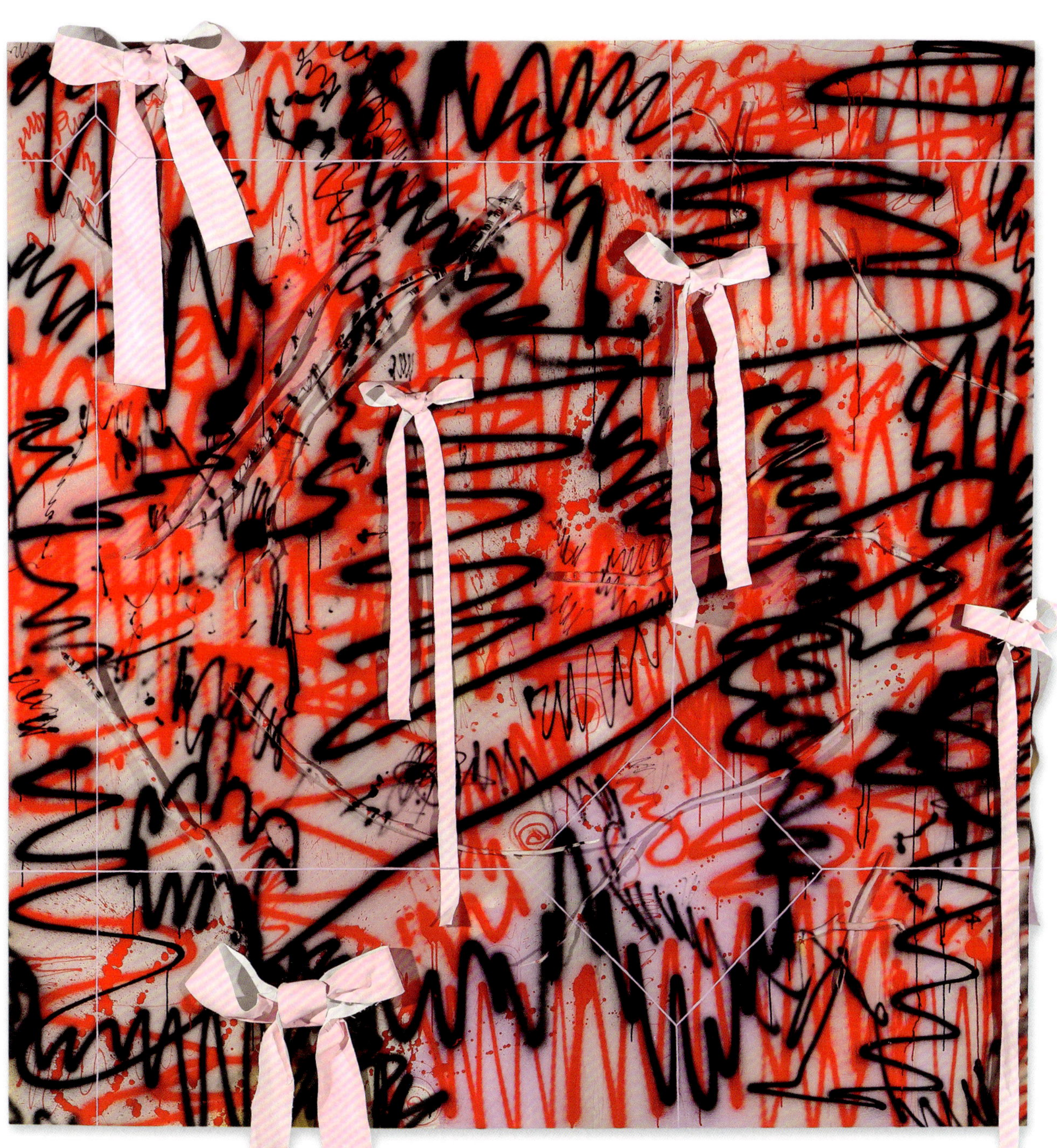

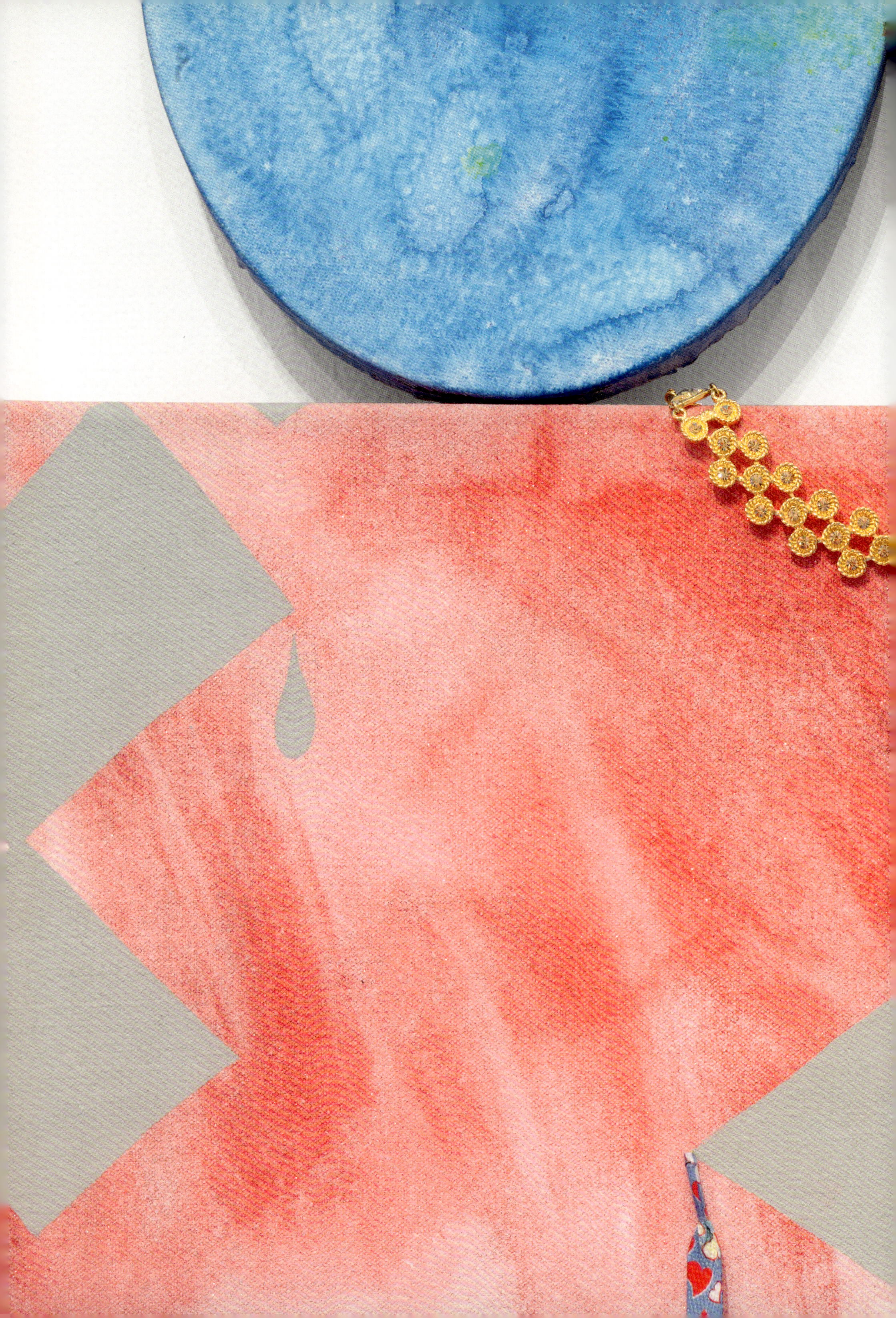

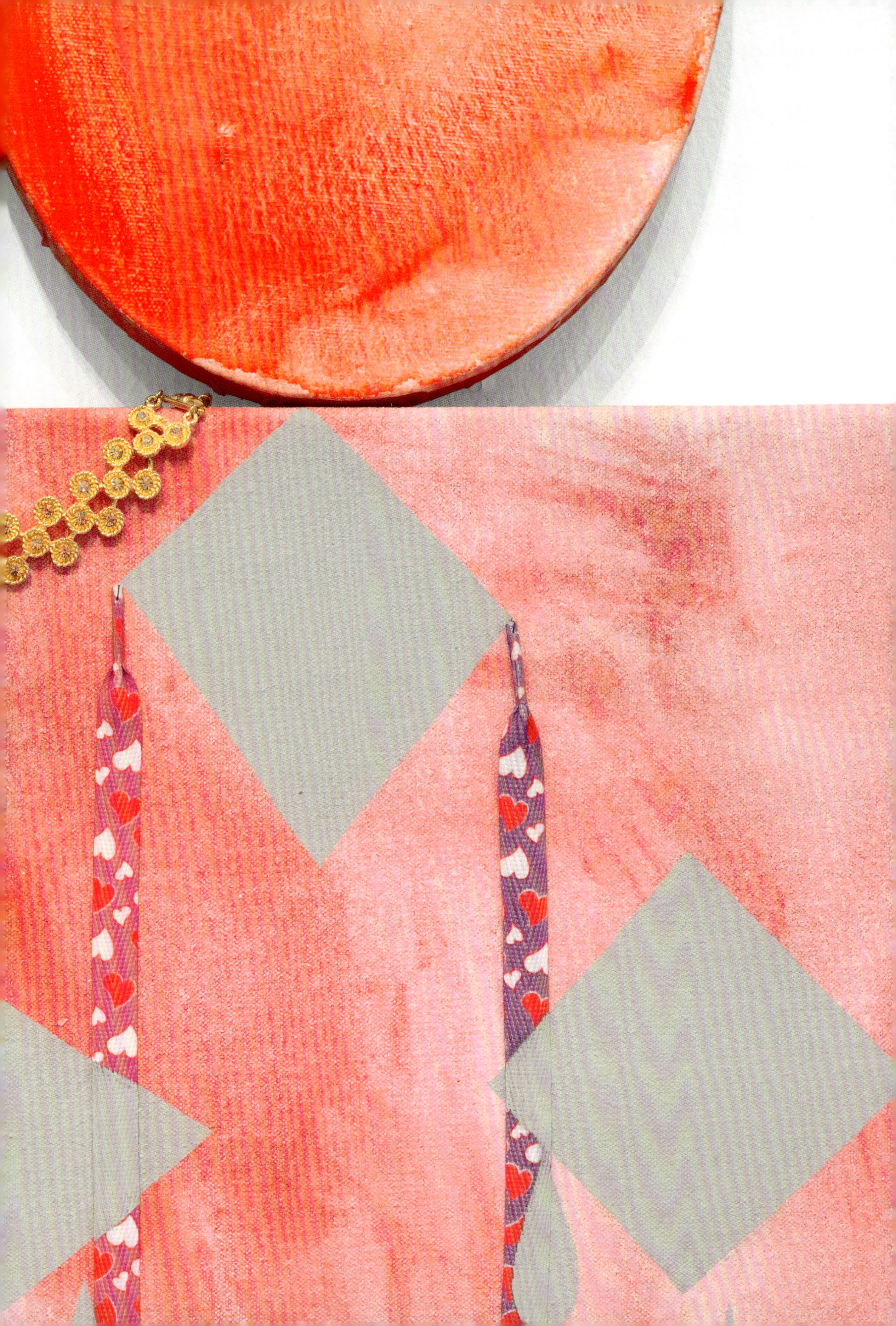

crying in public, 2012
(detail on preceding spread)

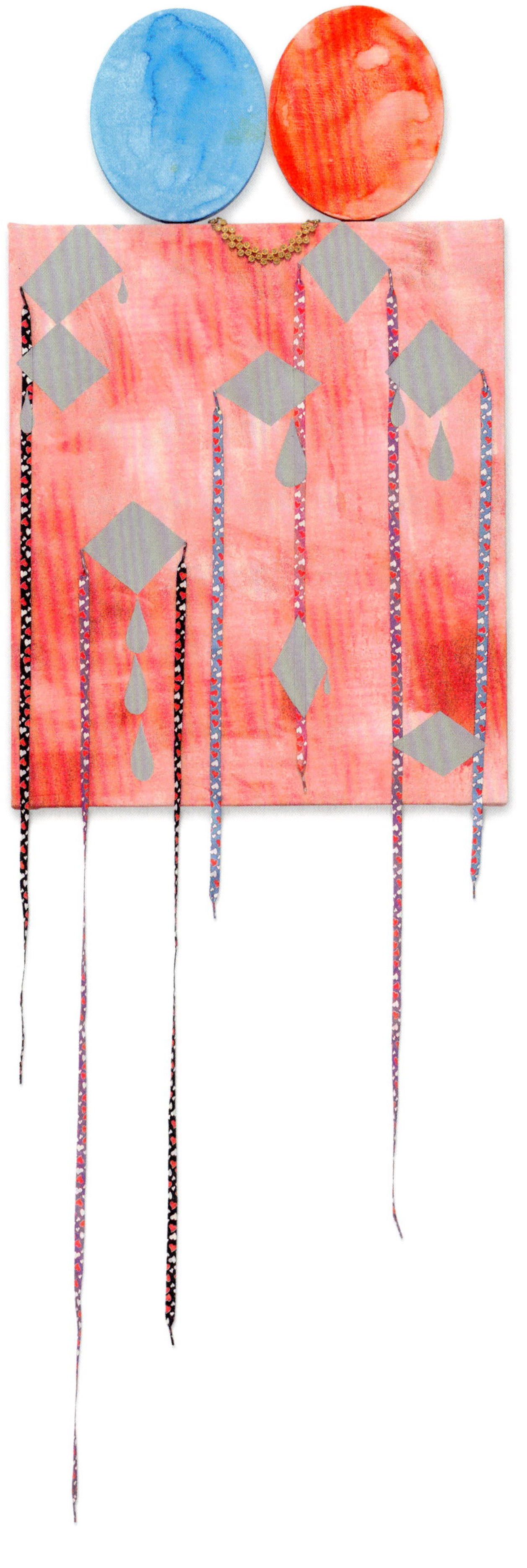

enter the center, 2016
(detail on following spread)

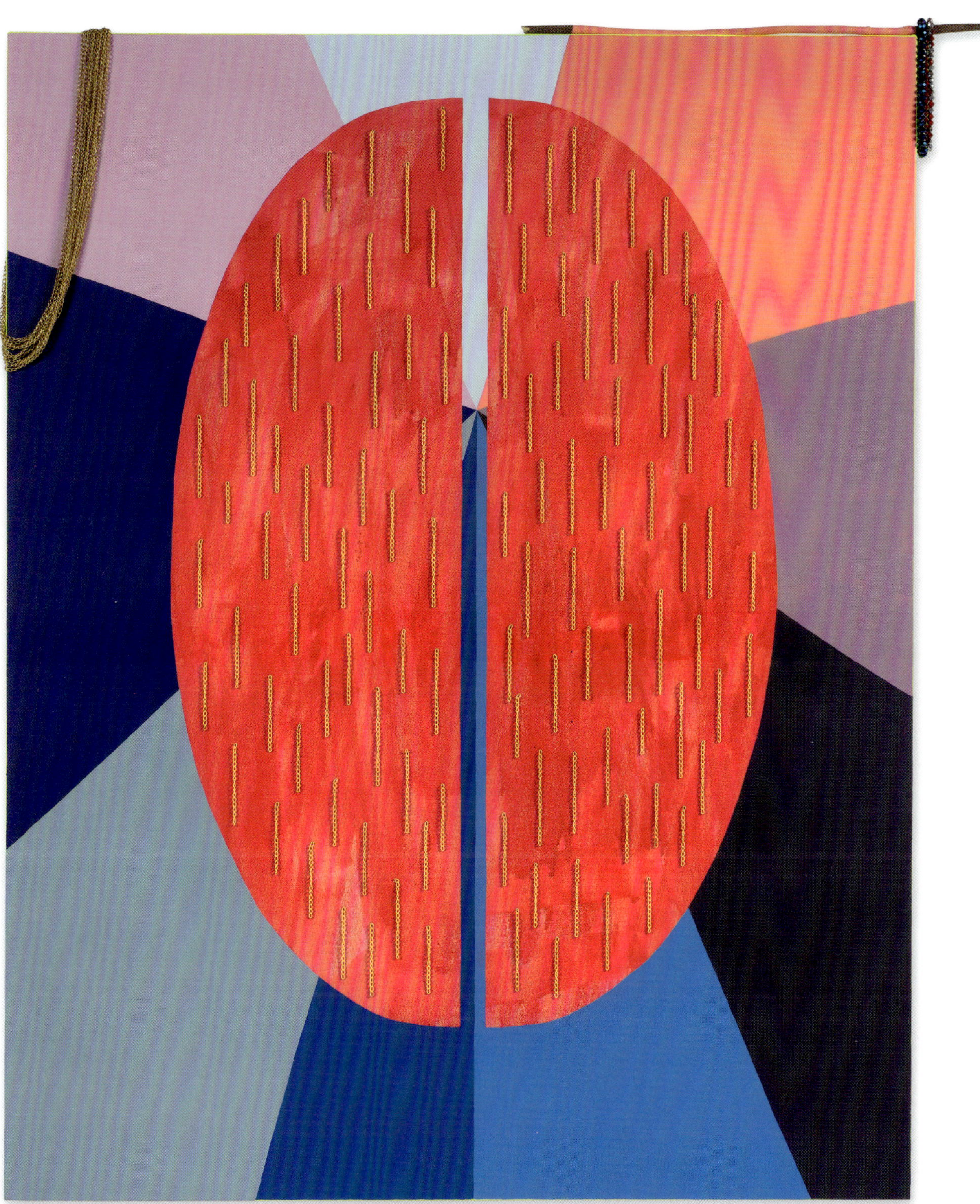

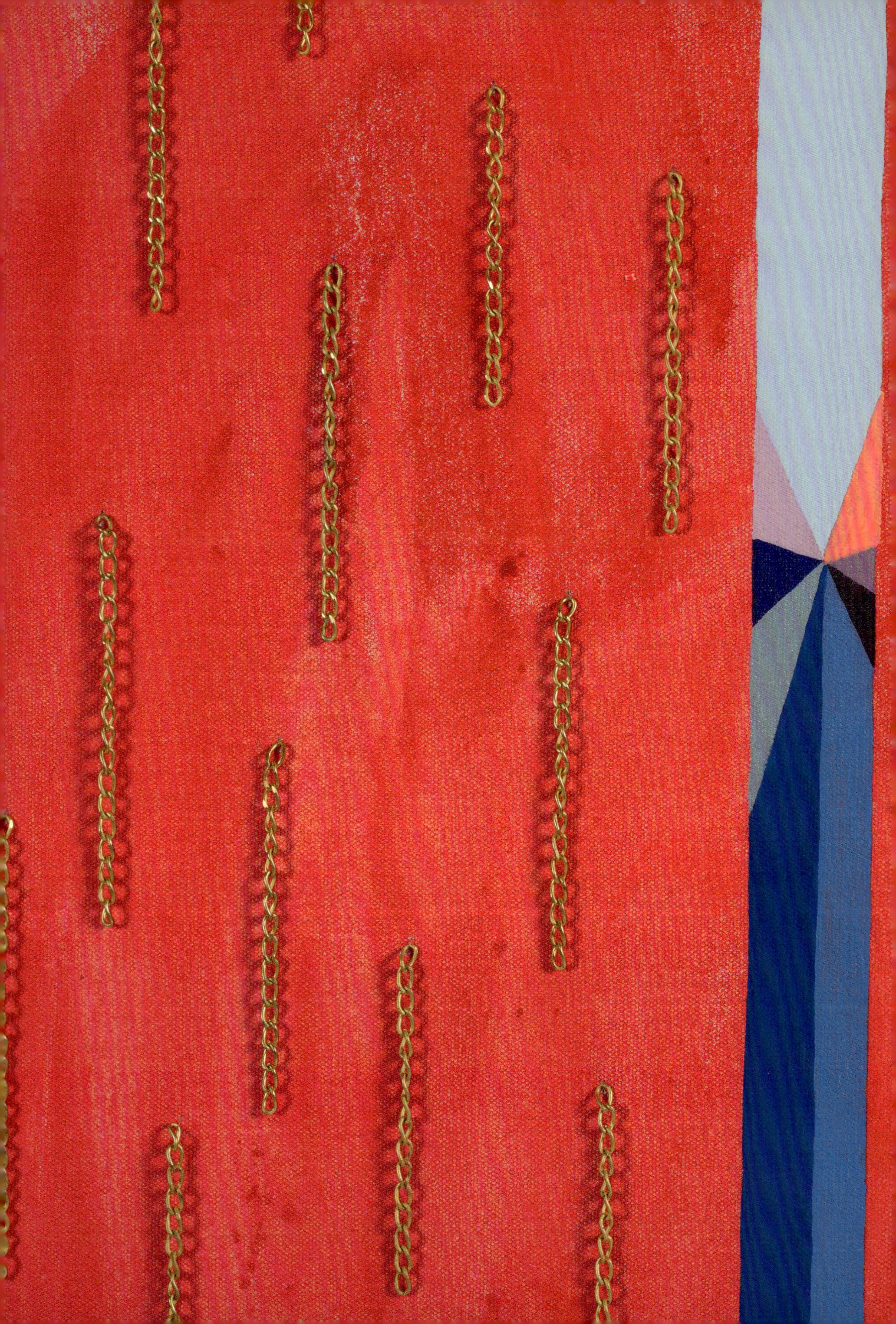

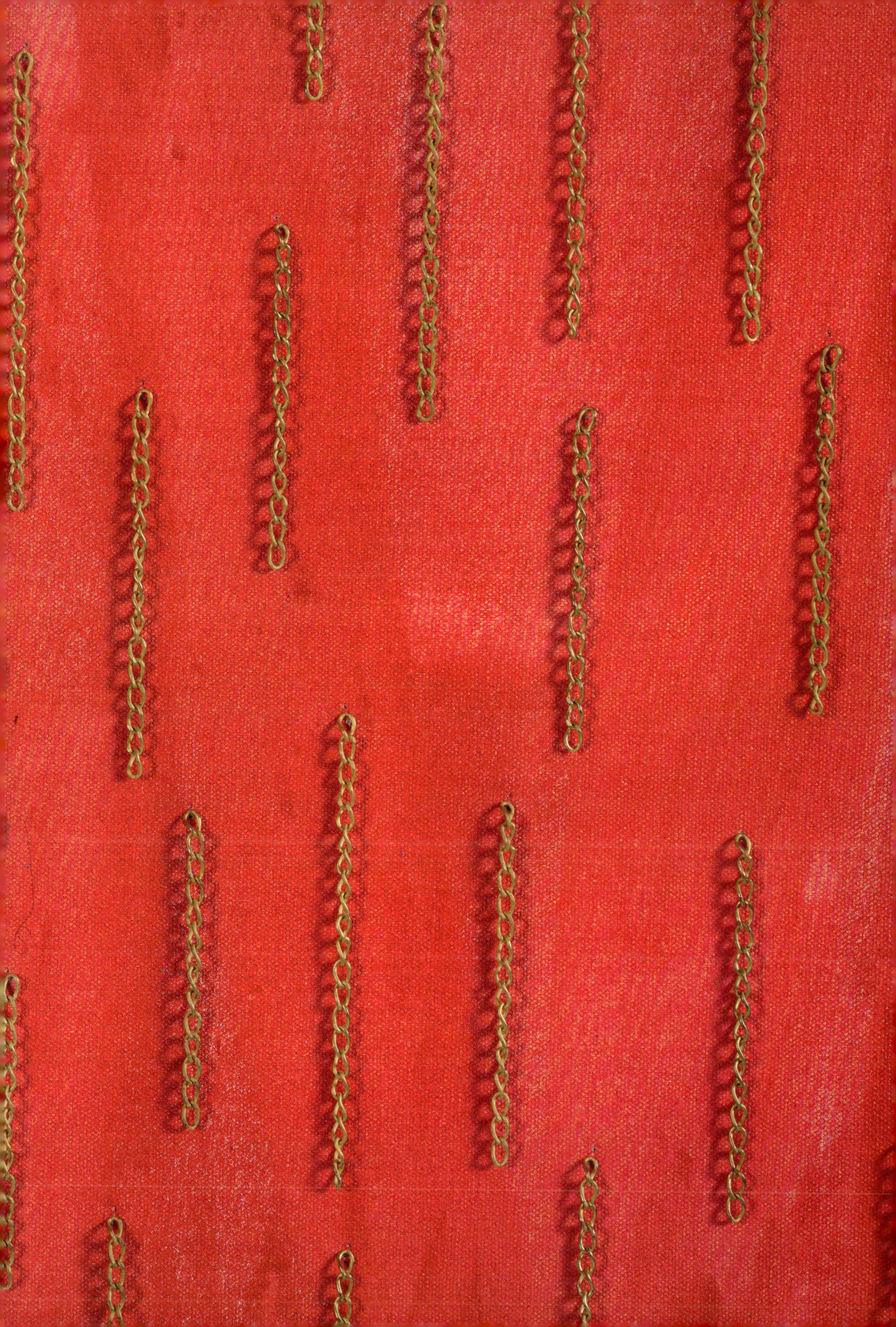

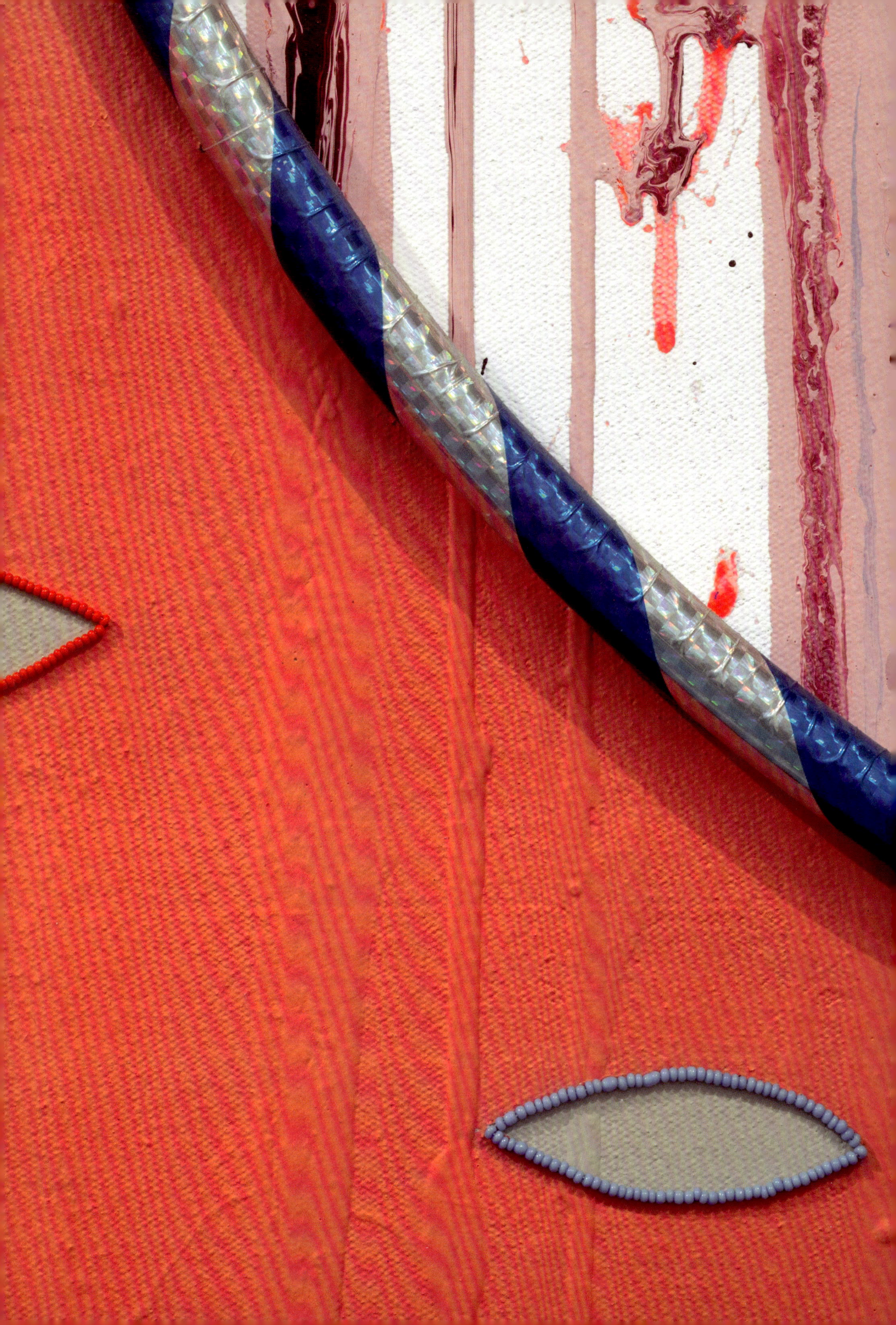

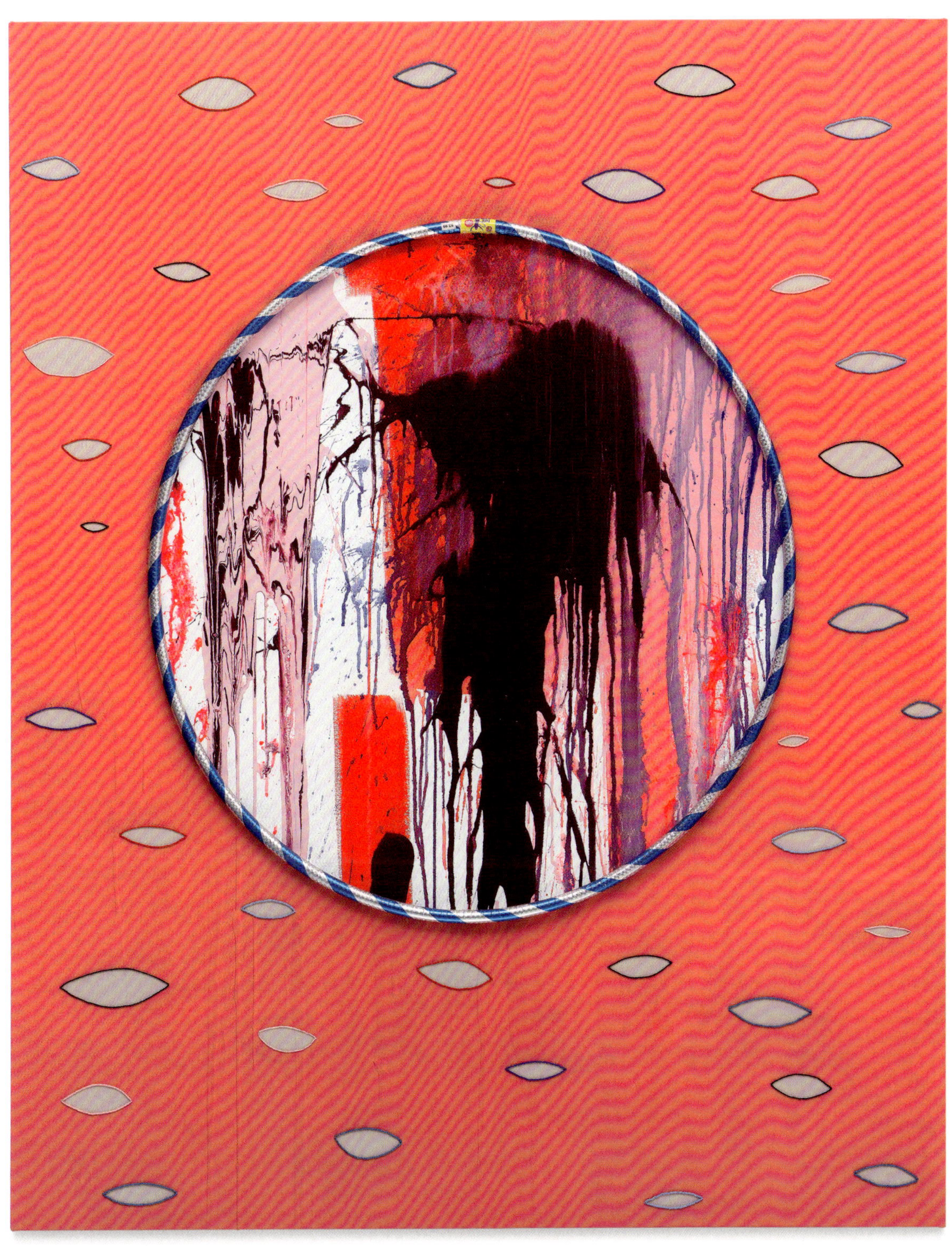

Glory, 2014
(detail facing)

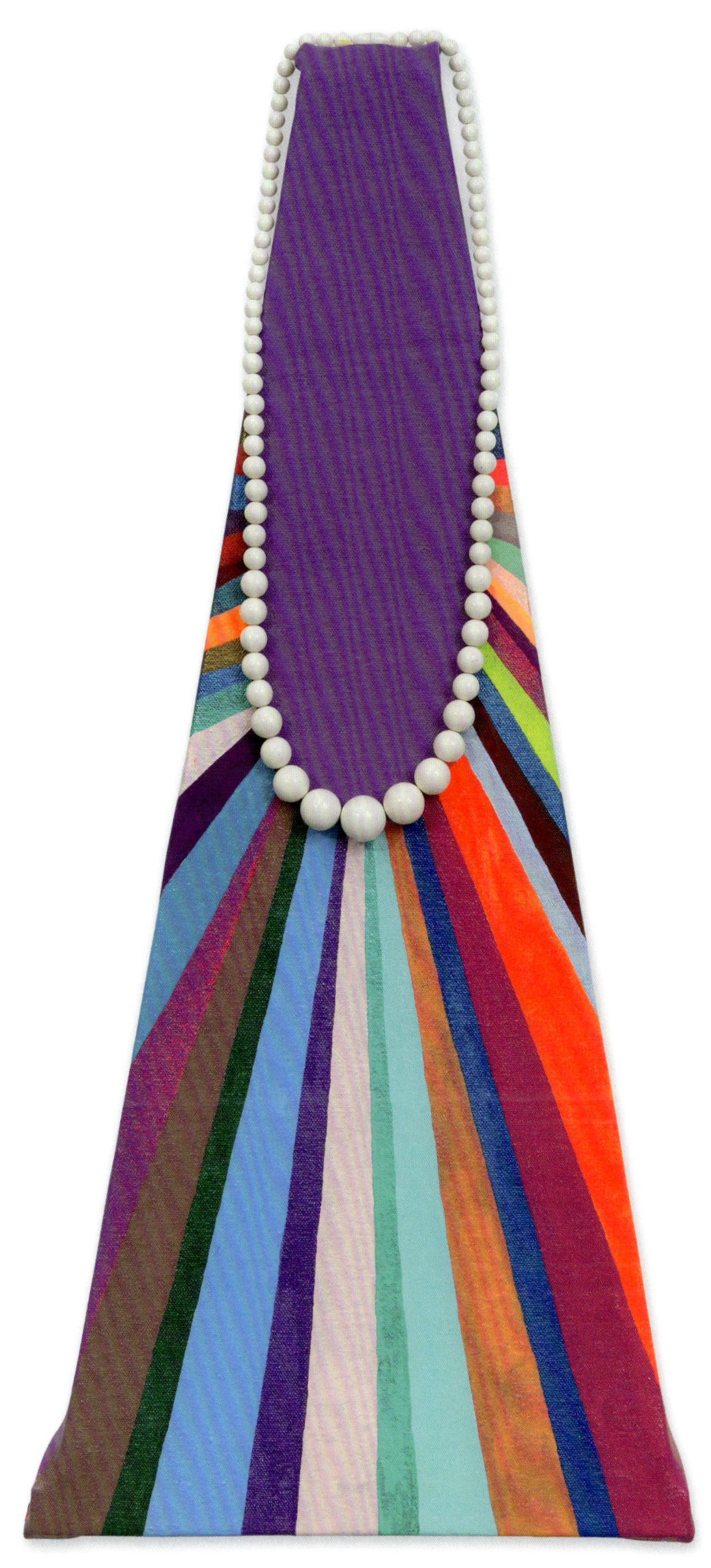

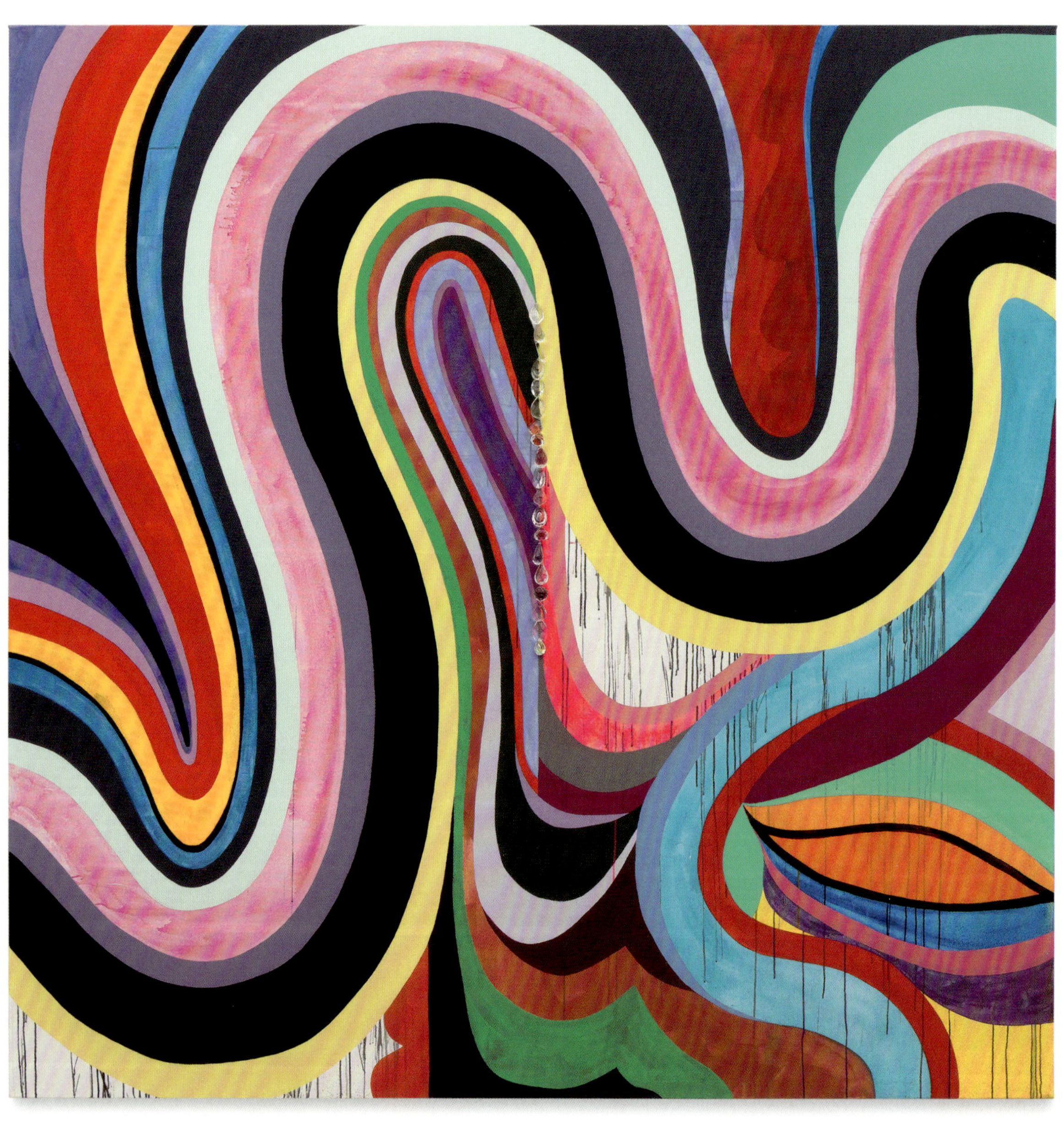

Self Portrait, 2020
(detail facing)

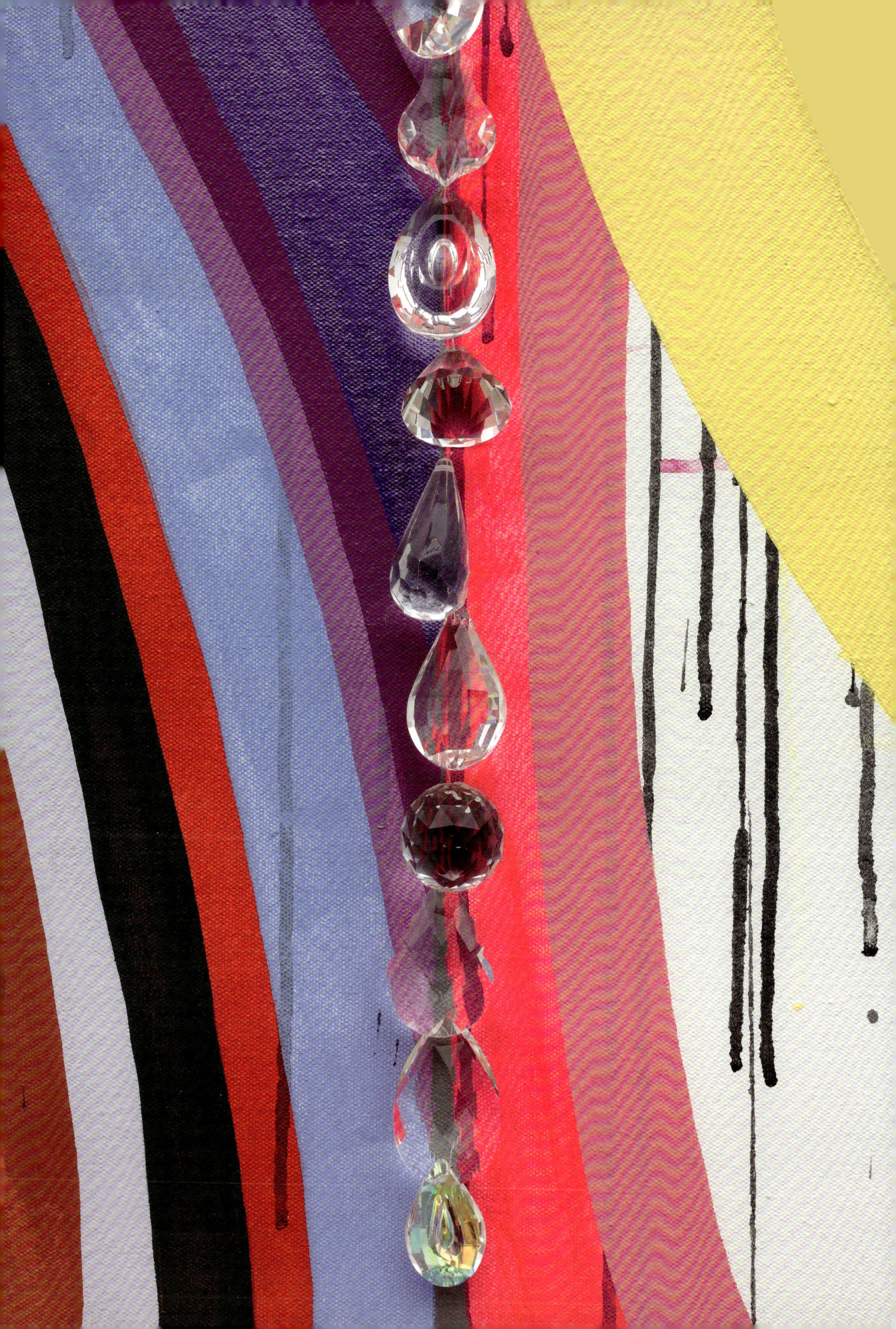

bras, 2017

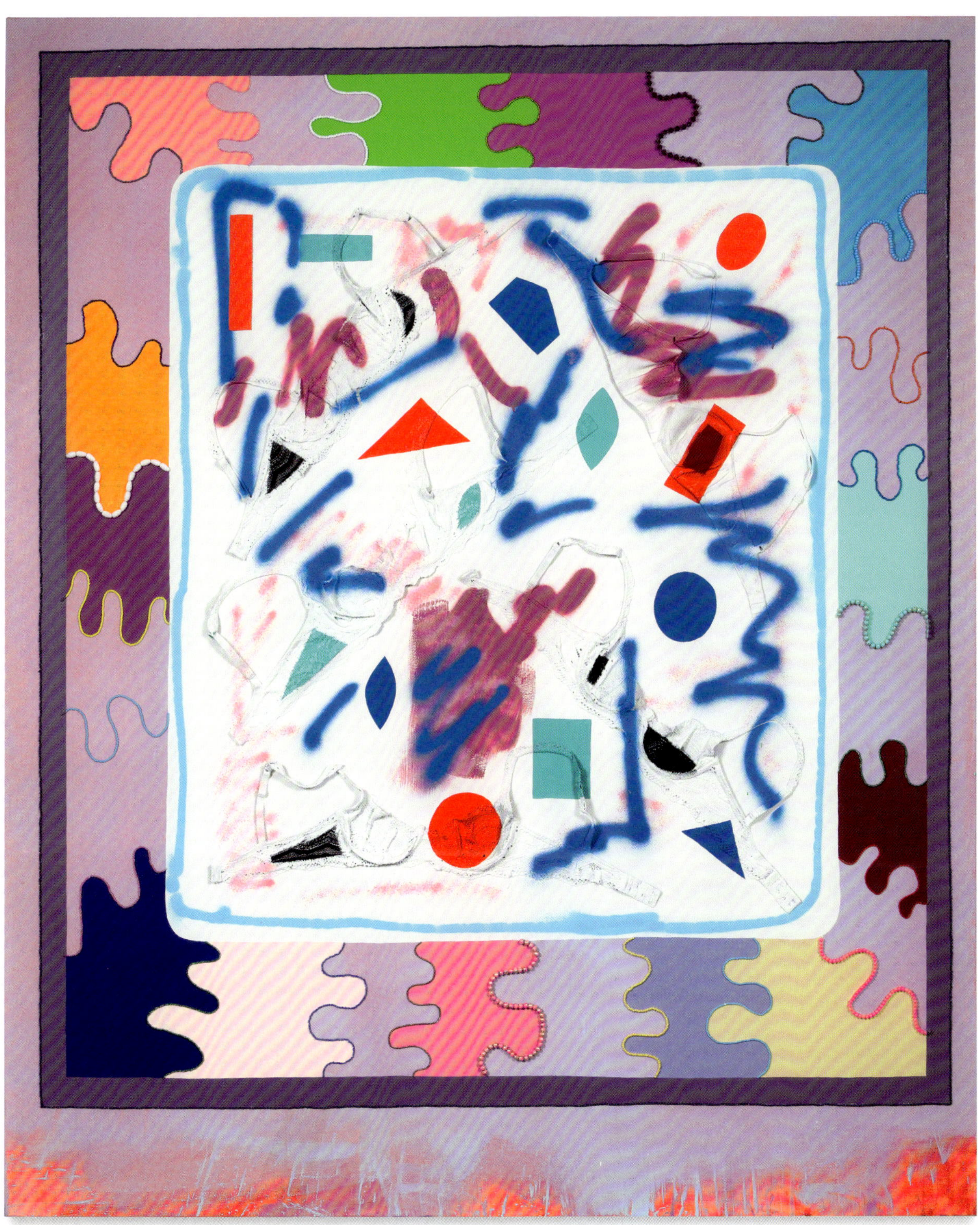

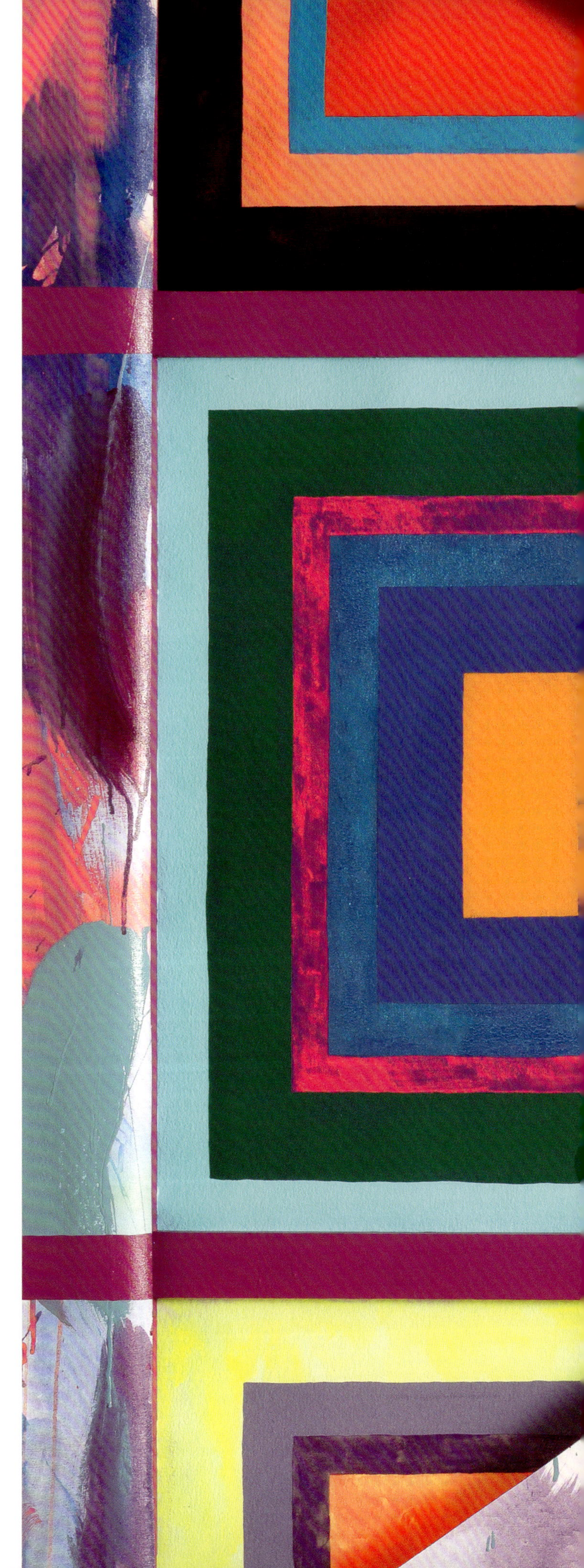

My favorite season is the fall of the patriarchy, 2020, (detail)
following spread, installation view:
National Gallery of Art, Washington DC, 2021

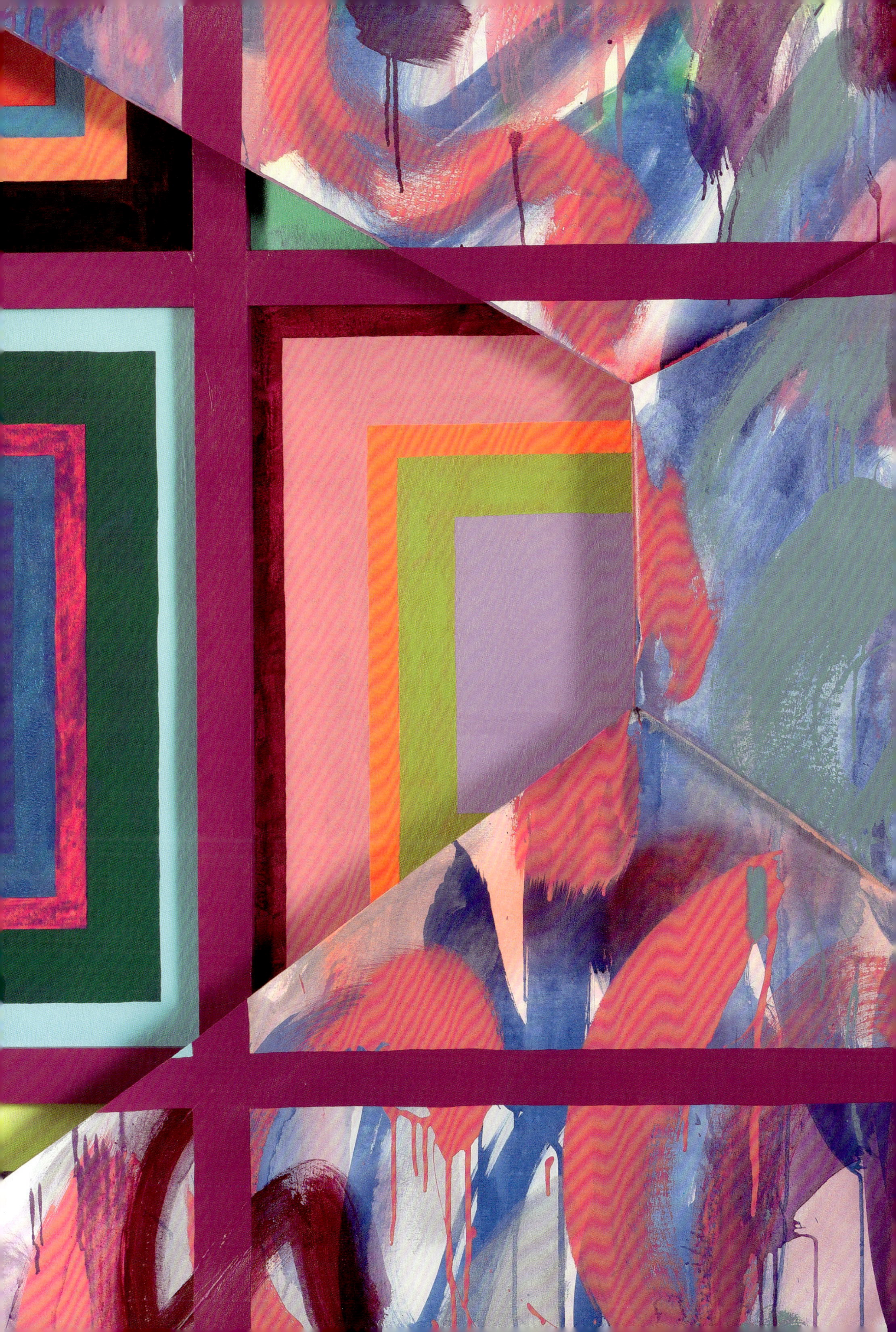

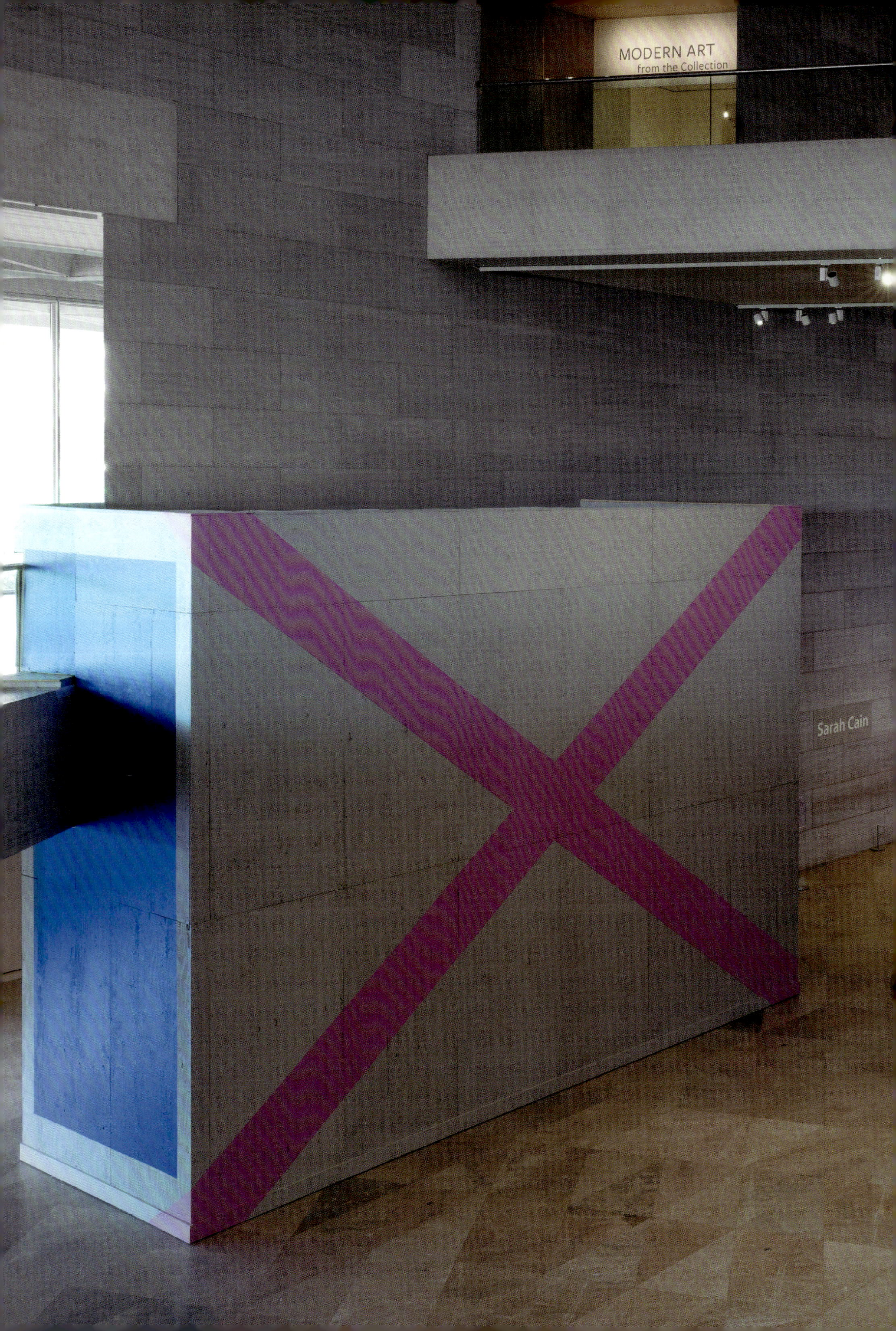
MODERN ART
from the Collection
Sarah Cain

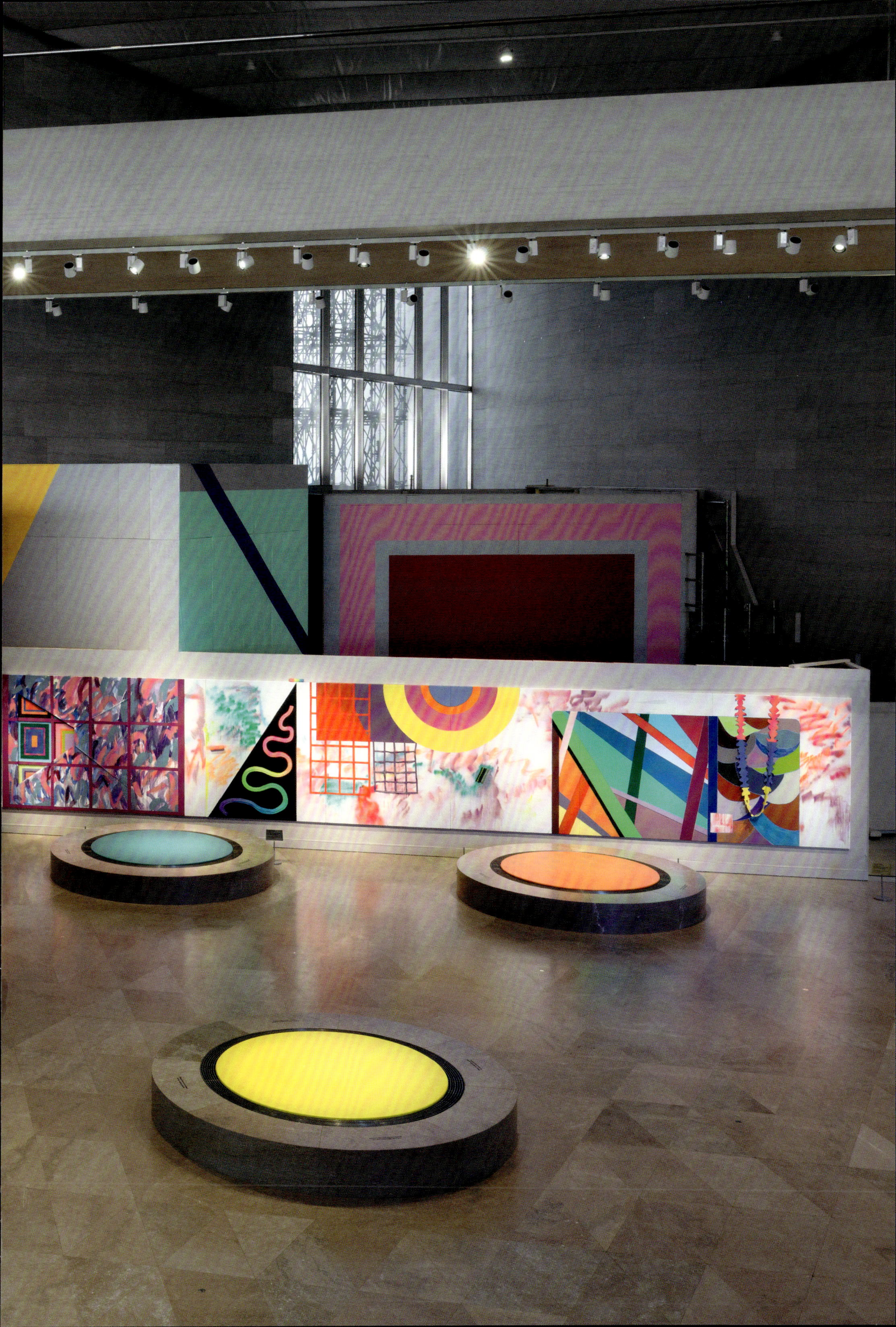

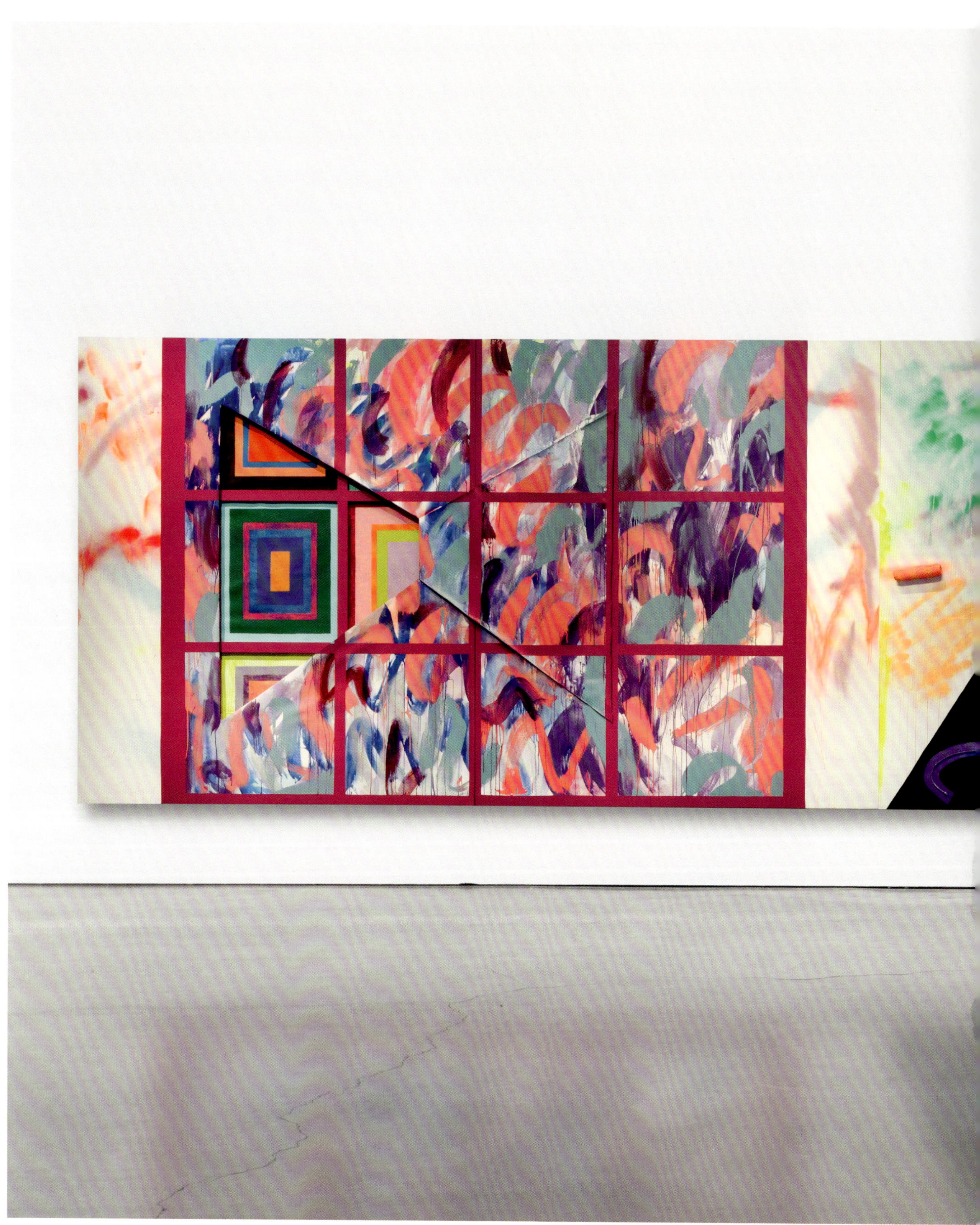

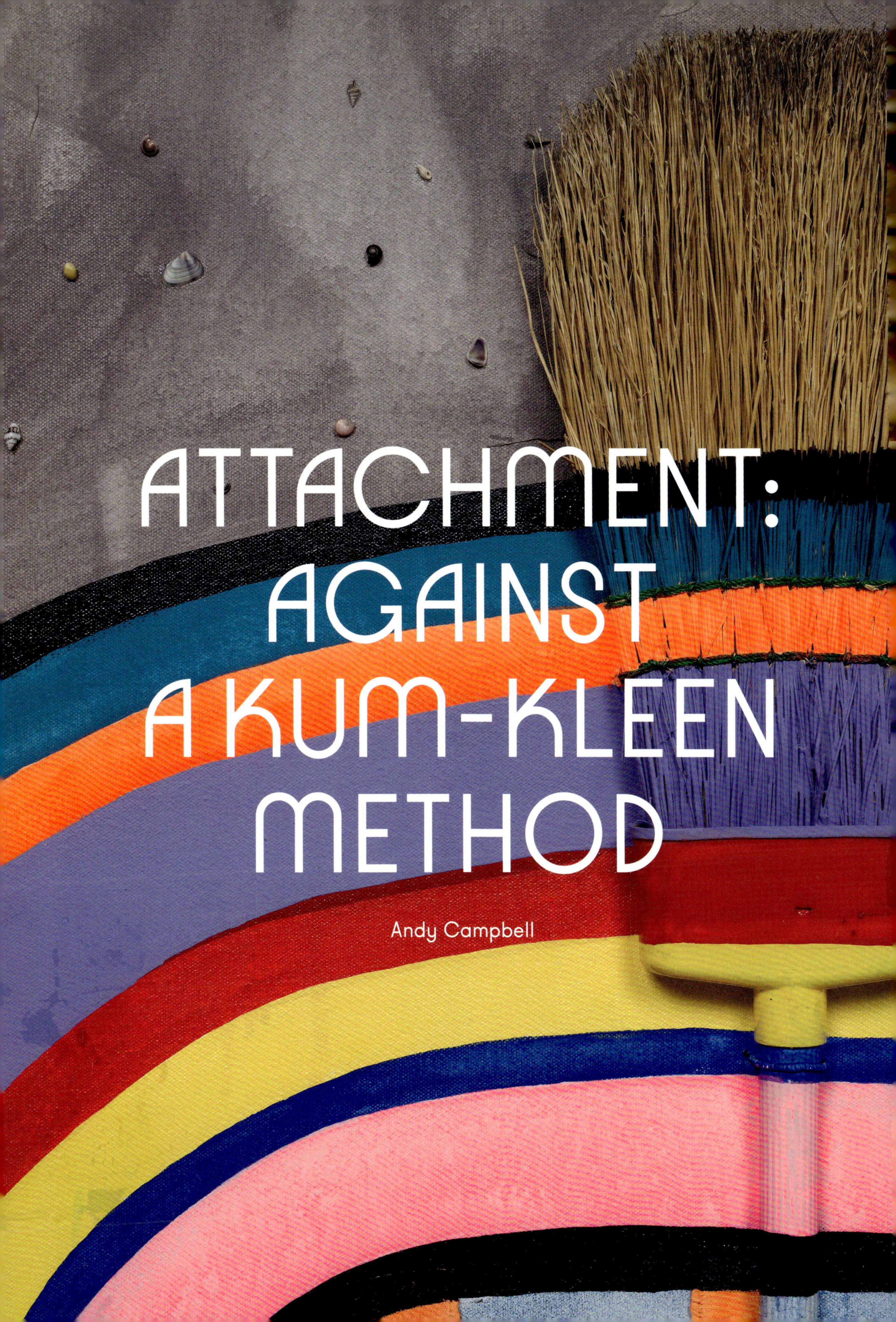
ATTACHMENT:
AGAINST
A KUM-KLEEN
METHOD
Andy Campbell

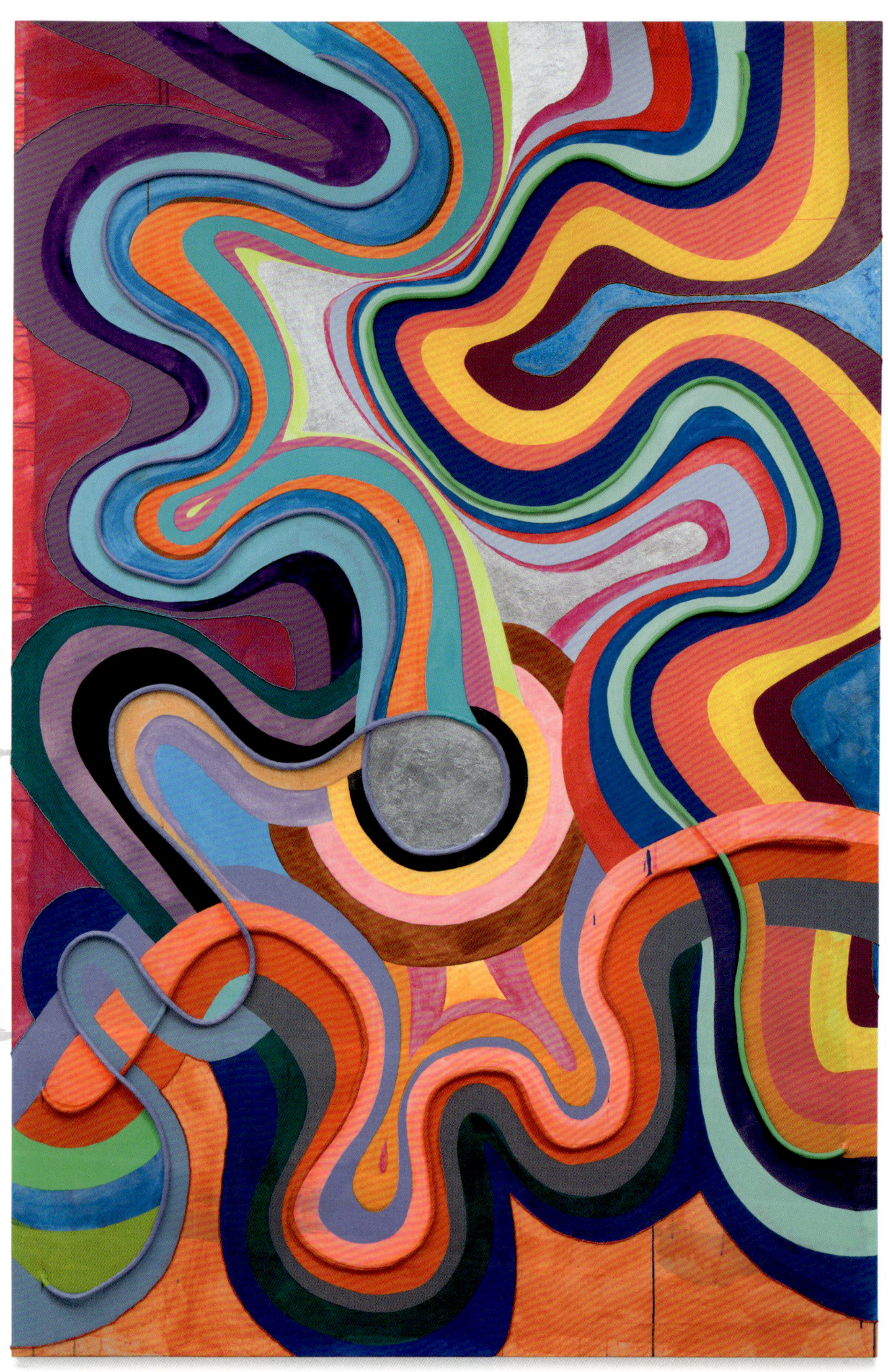

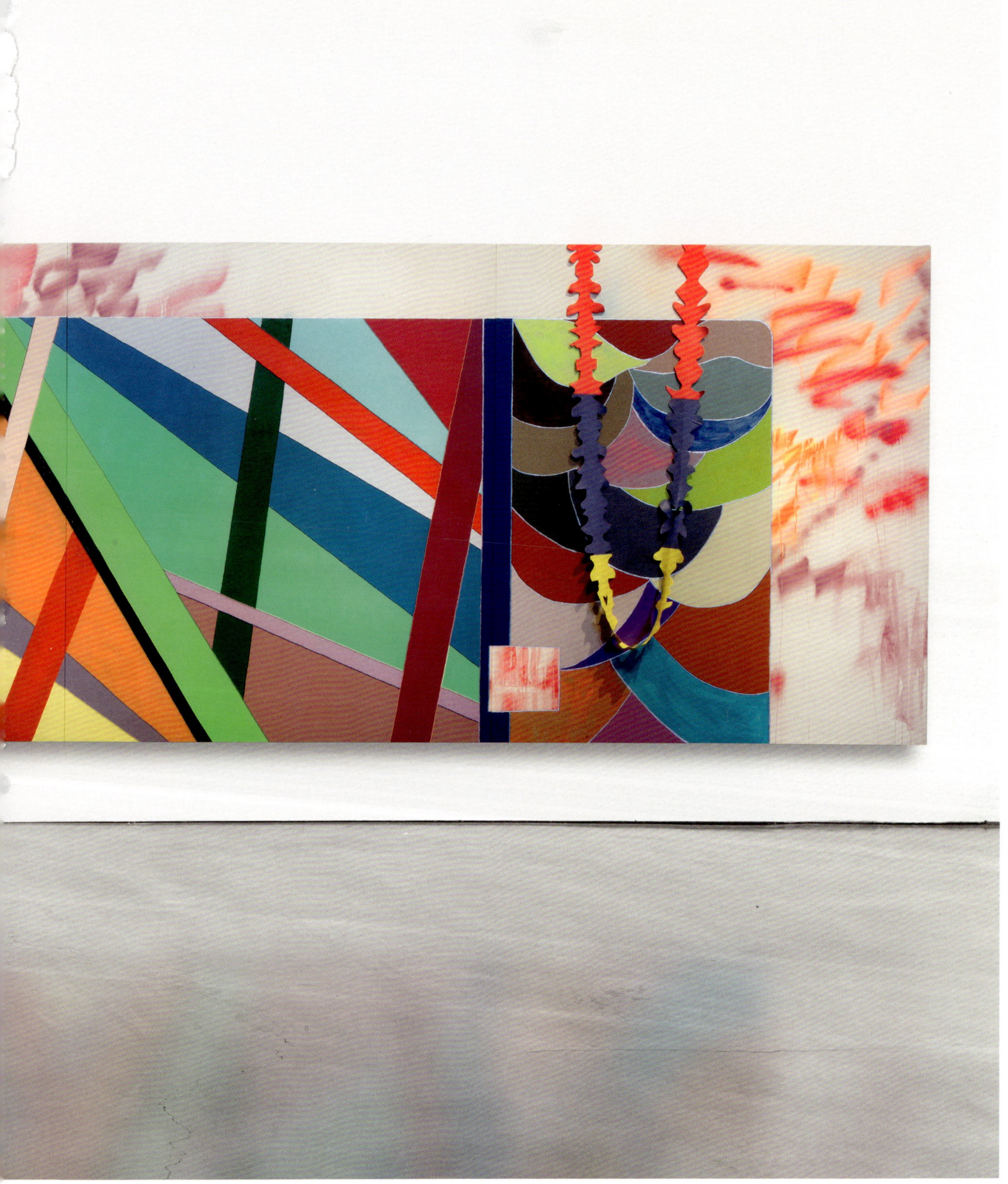

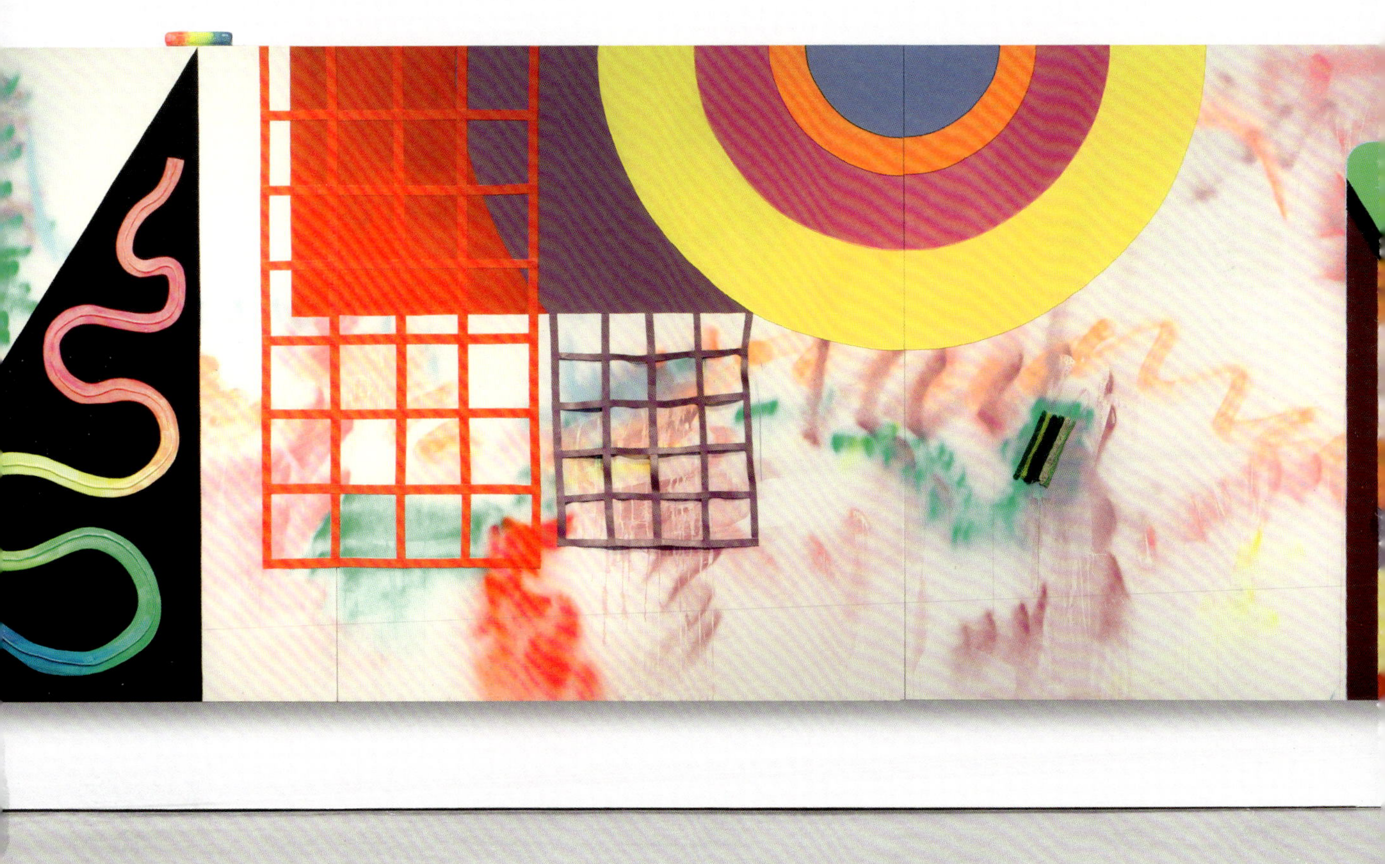

Walk in lightly, leave like lightning, 2022

Attachment, therefore, is a psychoanalytic concept related to
unconscious or unwilled fantasy investment, an affective
concept tracking attachments to situations exemplifying forms of
life, a concern of ideology critique by way of the selling
of normativity, and a phenomenal practice of being an object
thrown into the world with other objects. To politicize attachment
requires attending to, and proposing continuities among
multiple subjectivities, thinking that they're organized in relation
to the same object, scene, or problem, even if the object,
scene, or problem that we think is collectively organizing is really
a magnet for heterogenous forces and fantasies.
—Lauren Berlant[2]

◊◊◊

I write to you in the aftermath of *attachment*, ongoing.

But before you get too excited … girlhood.

Or—for some of us—boyhood.

Anchored belonging: what was promised? and to whom?

Now, ask it from the other side: who *hasn't* been betrayed by their attachments?

This question issues from Lauren Berlant's quadripartite definition of attachment above. For Berlant—whose recent death underlines how one can continue to be "thrown into the world," even when, in some basic, awful sense, one is out of it—attachments at once make new things possible, and also present obdurate stoppages in the ways that we feel (or assume ourselves to be) in league with others via citizenship, genre, and normativity.

As for betrayal, I can't pinpoint the first time it happened to me. [As if it was something external—wrong!]. Nor am I able to coherently catalogue and order all the betrayals I've instigated, lived though, and taken on. And yet I know it is not possible to survive without them.

But here's the thing about betrayals: they bleed and become attachments themselves. Here the anterior is also the interior of whatever comes after (and to some extent, whatever came before).

Keeping an eye on your attachments (and betrayals) presents the possibility of an oscillating focus, persisting in the world in many forms, but specifically for this essay: as painting, reading.

I offer this as a way of recognizing the decisions that go into making Sarah Cain's paintings. So I'll focus on one kind of decision that happens many times across her work, which is to attach something to something else.

Shoelaces. Feathers. A clutch of beads. Coat hangers. Prisms of varying complexity, size, and colors.

Cain refers to them all as "add-ons."[3]

[Women in Power]

◊◊◊

Like others I know, sometimes I want to describe and be charged by an atmosphere.

Even so: free radicals—a cat's stray hair floating onto a wet painting, for example—assert themselves.

A humid day makes work impossible;

Or, someone has misinterpreted instructions, and there needs to be clarification;

Or an affordance must be made—a curt push or resigned acceptance;

Or, you just can't get your mind off X;
     (man . . . fuck X!)

Or, an earthquake, because you live in California.

It's not always so dark or dire, sometimes you simply don't feel like it.

◊◊◊

Sometimes you end things before, or shortly after treading down an unhelpful path.

A previous version of this essay attempted (poorly) to mimic the form of a dictionary. The idea was to describe and therefore categorize the kinds of mechanical attachments evident in the making of Sarah Cain's paintings, thereby getting to attachments of a more non-mechanical kind. The entries were rendered in the past tense, giving the false impression that the work of attachment was somehow done or over: chained, dangled, draped, glued, hung, hooked, leaned, nailed, pinned, sewn, stapled, suspended, threaded, and tied.

It's important to leave some evidence of what was before.

But of course, it is chaining, dangling, draping, gluing, hanging, hooking, leaning, nailing, pinning, sewing, stapling, suspending, threading, tying, and the combination of these strategies-in-the-present that is really the nut of Cain's paintings.

◊◊◊

"The problem of attachments is to both compose attachments and attend to them," says Kathleen Stewart in her dialogue with Lauren Berlant, "…of being open to the eventhood of the world."[4] Years after she said this, Stewart and Berlant published The Hundreds together, a collaborative sequence of one hundred hundred-word texts.

There, in a "hundred" titled "Refraction," they begin:

> An enigma that is also an overfilling of form renders its "we" a
> voice of contagious reiteration. A mystery path entrains a
> problematic, pressing materials into service. Some people become
> its crazy or a refraction of its tempo or some chaos of possibilities.[5]

The eventhood is here, remaining in elastic tension to our collected histories of betrayal.

And here I pause: writing an atmosphere might mean attending to particulates, and to the masses that move them. Dent into incident.[6]

So I am transmitting to you from an entered center—from the faceted interior of a smokey prism dangling on the edge of a curving, vertical void.

[Untitled (The Void)]

◊◊◊

The company known as Avery Dennison, which bills itself as a "global materials science company," (and trades under the acronym AVY on the New York Stock Exchange) could be partially responsible for an atmospheric relationship to attachment that those of us who lived through the sicker crazes of the 1970s + 1980s, one that continues to orient a certain way of thinking about the obligations we have (or don't have) to one another.

At its base, this is a story of removal (you'll note a very anti-add-on sentiment at work here); a fantasy of return to the way things used to be.

Back then—in 1935—Avery Dennison was known under a different name: Kum Kleen Products.[7] The adhesive stickers that were the company's only product promised what was so clearly indexed in the company's name. To come away 'cleanly'— or 'kleenly,' (which is clean, but not kwite)—without tearing or leaving a sticky film on whatever it was attached to.

Perhaps it will not surprise you that first stickers were made for the purpose of pricing. Unassuming standardized small round dots—similar in kind to the ones used today in yard and garage sales, or art fairs. The "kum-kleen technology," was an anticipated denouement to the narrative drama of the sale, upholding the belief that one might be able to remove any overt reminder of the context of transaction from daily life.

◊◊◊

The fact is we leave residue.

Everywhere there is evidence of our attachments

…and even though it means admitting that not only slimeballs leave a trail,

let's be done with the Kum-Kleen myth.

◊◊◊

[The Italians]

One way to think about what Sarah Cain does is chaining: linking things and actions in an atmosphere of making.

Take *The Italians* (2010), one work within a complex, site-responsive installation built over the course of a month in Sarah Meltzer Gallery, a former garment manufactory. The show was titled "California Does Psychic," and dedicated, in a fundamental way, to the experimental strategies of New York *L=A=N=G=U=A=G=E* poet Hannah Weiner.

The Italians is comprised of a large canvas, whose relation to the floor and a nearby structural pillar (to which it seems to be attached) is crucial to understanding the formal strategies enacted in the painting. On one side of the painting colorful, vertical stripes course down from a diagonal slicing across the bottom third of the canvas and onto to the floor. If not a hinge in material fact, then certainly one in visual regard.

As with many of the other interventions in "California Does Psychic," this draws attention to the wear of the space—its "rawness"—a soft asset in exhibiting a certain kind of art.

An aside: this is not unrelated to some of Cain's earliest installation work, which was executed in Bay Area squats—time and human-smoothed spaces populated in the midst of corporate/city development. In these installations sometimes she would pick up whatever was handy—a blouse, for example—and by painting and hanging it on the wall, she could shift the whole idea of what was valuable in speculative capitalism.

[*In the eve of change*]

Back to *The Italians*, or rather to *The Italians*'s fabulous backside. Here, the painting's stretcher bars are visible—at points blending in with the bisecting green + yellow, and red + white fields of painterly activity, and in other places painted a stark white. A structure both acquiescing and refusing to fit in.

Breeching the difference between these two sides is a golden chain, which hangs in two catenaries on the painting's front. In the back it is threaded coyly behind the painting's vertical stretcher bar, its ends dangling on the extremities of the painting's width.

The chain, for me, is an indicator of how to be with this particular painting, an invitation to hang out between its front and back, to look in loops that trail off onto the floor or into space. Material and atmospheric, it describes the possibilities of attachment—from the intimacy of being tucked away to the ferocity of taking up more space than anyone rightly or wrongly "gave" you.

◊◊◊

[Mister]

Writing about Cain's add-ons, this is how one reviewer gets it wrong: "[…] goofiness— and girliness—enter the picture, disrupting the muscularity of Cain's compositions."[8]

No.

Goofiness and girliness *are the muscles* trained in patriarchy's horrid gymnasium.

They exist as an ambient threat that many still refuse to fully attune to.

Knotted ribbons, beaded hearts, dangling chains…a shared and precious code for fuck you.

See? Betrayal.

◊◊◊

[crying in public]

Sometimes an add-on is also a fake-out. *crying in public* (2012) is a good example.

Two ovoid paintings, one red—one blue, rest atop a canvas populated with greyed-out diamond shapes and teardrops. Drooping shoelaces (each sewn carefully and decisively through its plastic aglet to the canvas ground) dangle comically past the lower terminus of the painting, amplifying the downward orientation that an act of crying suggests. Tears streaming down and fallen spirits.

The shoelaces are patterned with red and white hearts, and when one intersects with a diamond or teardrop shape Cain overpaints it in grey, as though situating the stuff of the world in the infrathin space between gesso and paint.

Anyway, the red and blue paintings at the top are only attached to the larger canvas via another downward force, that of planetary gravity. From far away they seem to be connected to each other by a golden chain—really a bracelet, which gently (sweetly?) droops into the top of the painting. Upon closer inspection the bracelet doesn't really connect the oval canvases. Nothing does.

They touch—grounding one another in mutual dependence—and maybe that is enough at the end of any given day.

When moving *crying in public* from one place to another—as doubtless it needed to be crated, moved, and unpacked to get to The Tang for "Enter the Center"—its component pieces are always at risk of being separated. What is crying in public but an intensification of attachment against the fact of its putative loss? This threat haunts the painting, and maybe then seen in this light it turns the work's existence into a miracle of earth's force, human attention, and the strength of thread and paint.

I'm pretty sure this isn't the only work by Sarah Cain that this is true for.

◊◊◊

Let's braid, instead.

Let's knit in turn with others.

Let's keep a part of ourselves alive and secret

even when forced to hang against most blah backdrop.

Let's turn the feminization of togethering toward our benefit and find a space where we can attach and untangle at will.

Bending/bent in a certain way.

Let's braid, instead.

[French braid]

◊◊◊

Here's another way out, offered by Sarah Ahmed:

> For where emotions allow us to become attached to forms of
> community based on violence against others, they may allow us to
> become attached to forms of living in which the proximity of others is
> welcomed without condition, a welcoming that does read the failure of
> recognition as a form of violence or injury (and that does not convert
> such others into 'unlikeness'). Such a welcoming can only avoid
> becoming another form of appropriation if we assume that one cannot
> feel what the other feels, and that one cannot inhabit her body.[9]
> (Ahmed, 22)

◊◊◊

My comments here, brief though they may be, are an attempt to provide some room
for your own attachments, to give attention to a meagre few of the ways that
Sarah Cain manages material, and to pick at some places where we might fall into
league with our world and each other.

Berlant describes an object as a "cluster of promises to you."[10]

They seem to be warning us, naming an over-active, yet familiar fault-line.

Here find a dialogue about grief (and every now and then, reward)—

—a crystal spine refracting our worlds.

[self-portrait]

1 Pope.L "**DeaR 'Young' Artist," in *Social Medium: Artists Writing, 2000–2015*, edited by Jennifer Liese
(Brooklyn, NY: Paper Monument, 2016), 298.

2 Lauren Berlant and Kathleen Stewart, "Forms of Attachment: Affect at the Limits of the Political," dialogue, ICI Berlin
(July 9, 2012), web. https://www.ici-berlin.org/events/forms-of-attachment.

3 Tara McDowell, "Air as Cement," in *Sarah Cain*, edited LAND/Shamim M. Momin (Los Angeles, CA: LAND, 2012), 15.

4 Lauren Berlant and Kathleen Stewart, "Forms of Attachment," web.

5 Lauren Berlant and Kathleen Stewart, "Refractions," in *The Hundreds* (Durham, NC: Duke University Press, 2019), 120.

6 Lauren Berlant and Kathleen Stewart, "Forms of Attachment," web.

7 "Our Story," Avery Dennison Corporation, accessed August 18, 2021, https://www.averydennison.com/content
/corp/na/en/home/about-us/our_history.html.

8 David Pagel, "Review: Sarah Cain's 1,000-square-foot painting is just the start," *Los Angeles Times* (January 22, 2019),
web. https://www.latimes.com/entertainment/arts/la-et-cm-sarah-cain-review-20190122-story.html.

9 Sara Ahmed, "Communities that Feel: Intensity, Difference and Attachment," in Anu Koivunen and Susanna Paasonen
(eds.) *Affective Encounters: Rethinking Embodiment in Feminist Media Studies* (Turku, University of Turku 2000), 22.

10 Lauren Berlant and Kathleen Stewart, "Forms of Attachment," web.

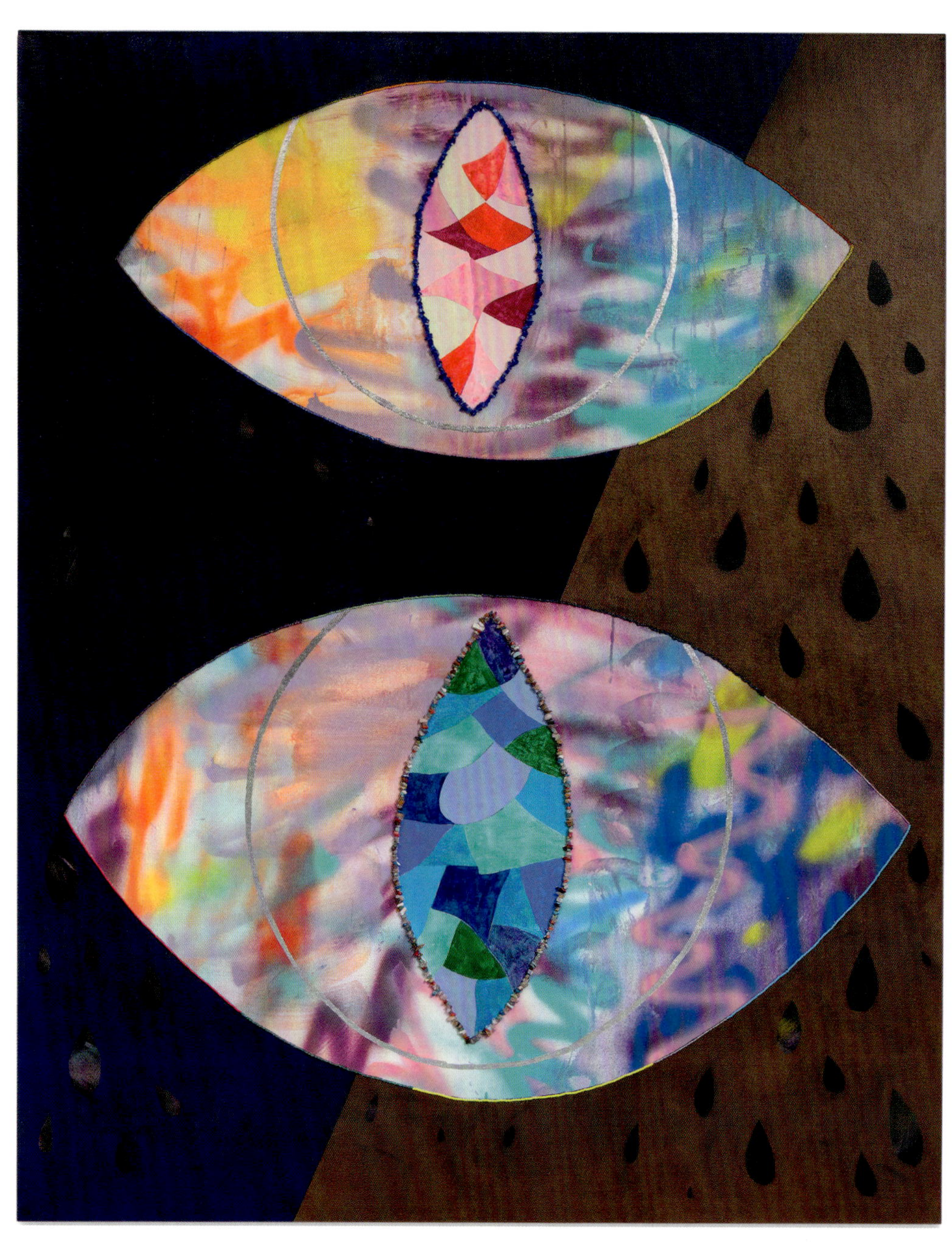

Crying Cat Eyes, 2018
(detail facing)

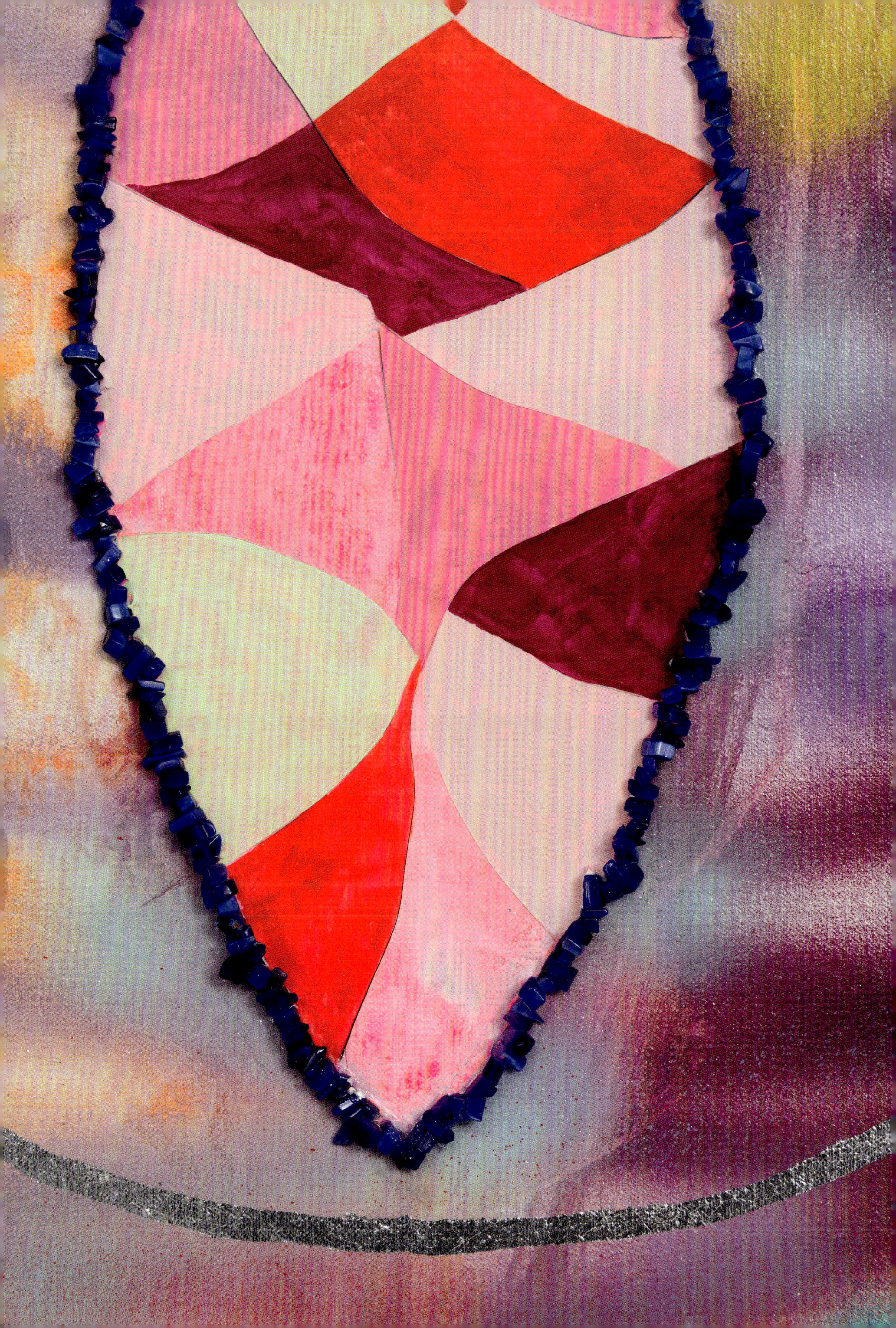

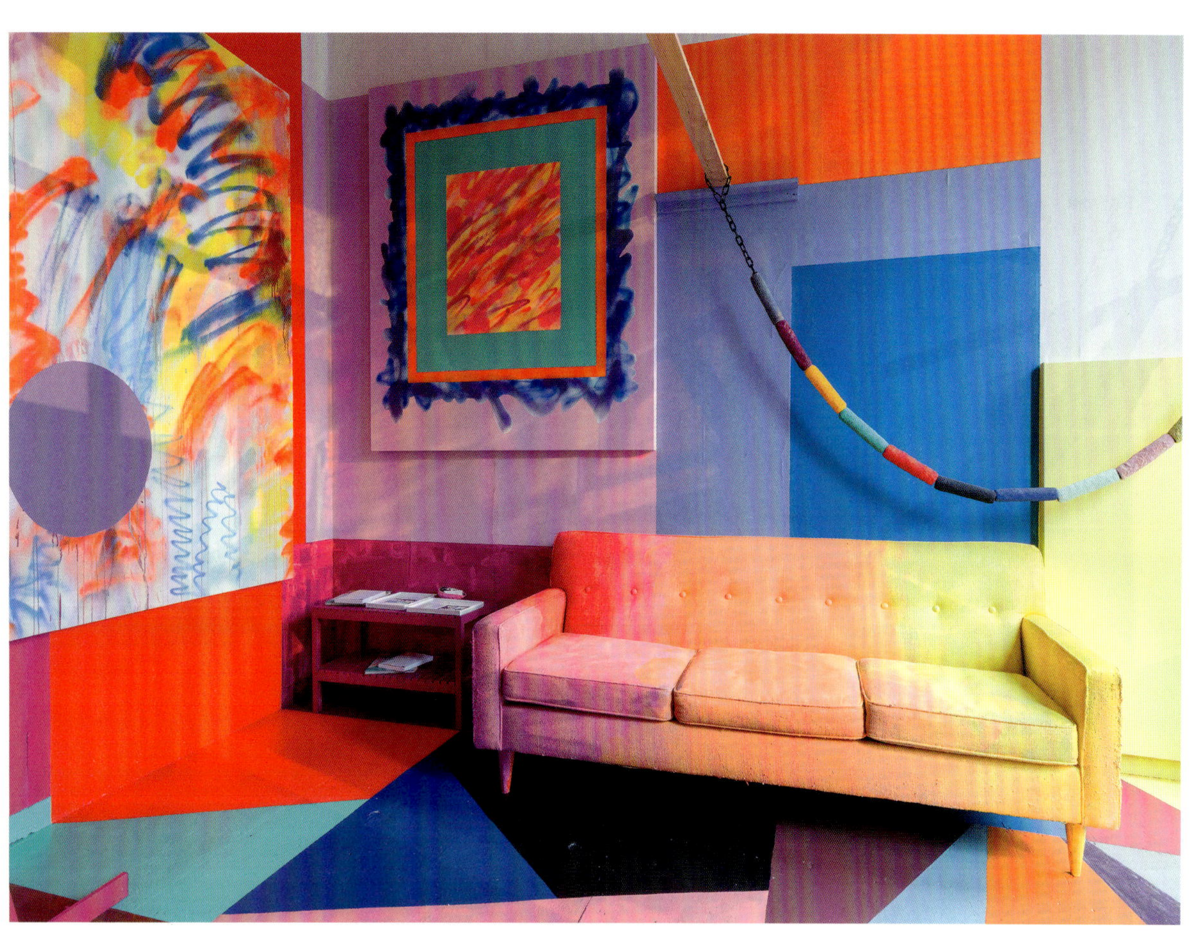

I touched a cactus flower, Frieze Los Angeles, 2019

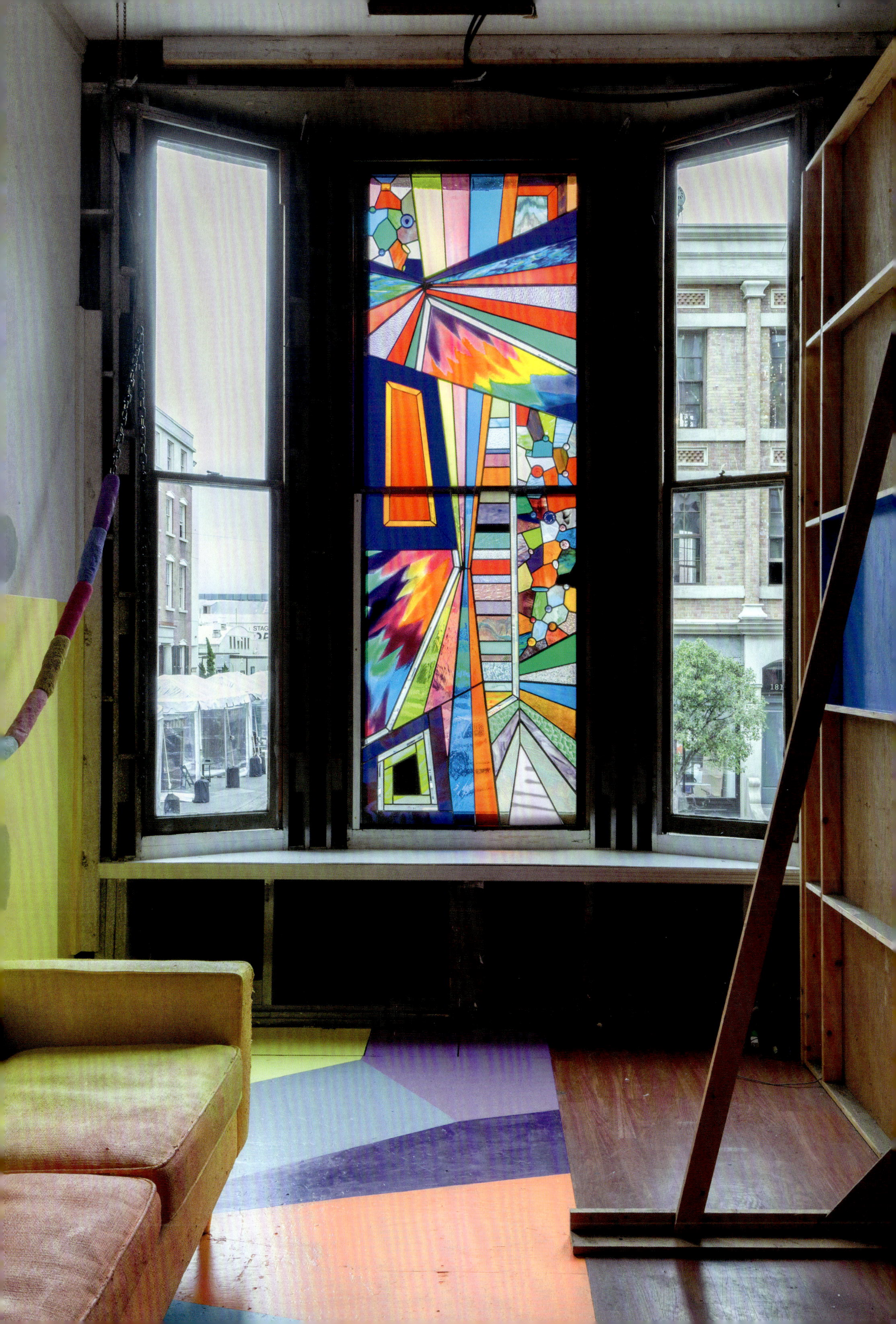

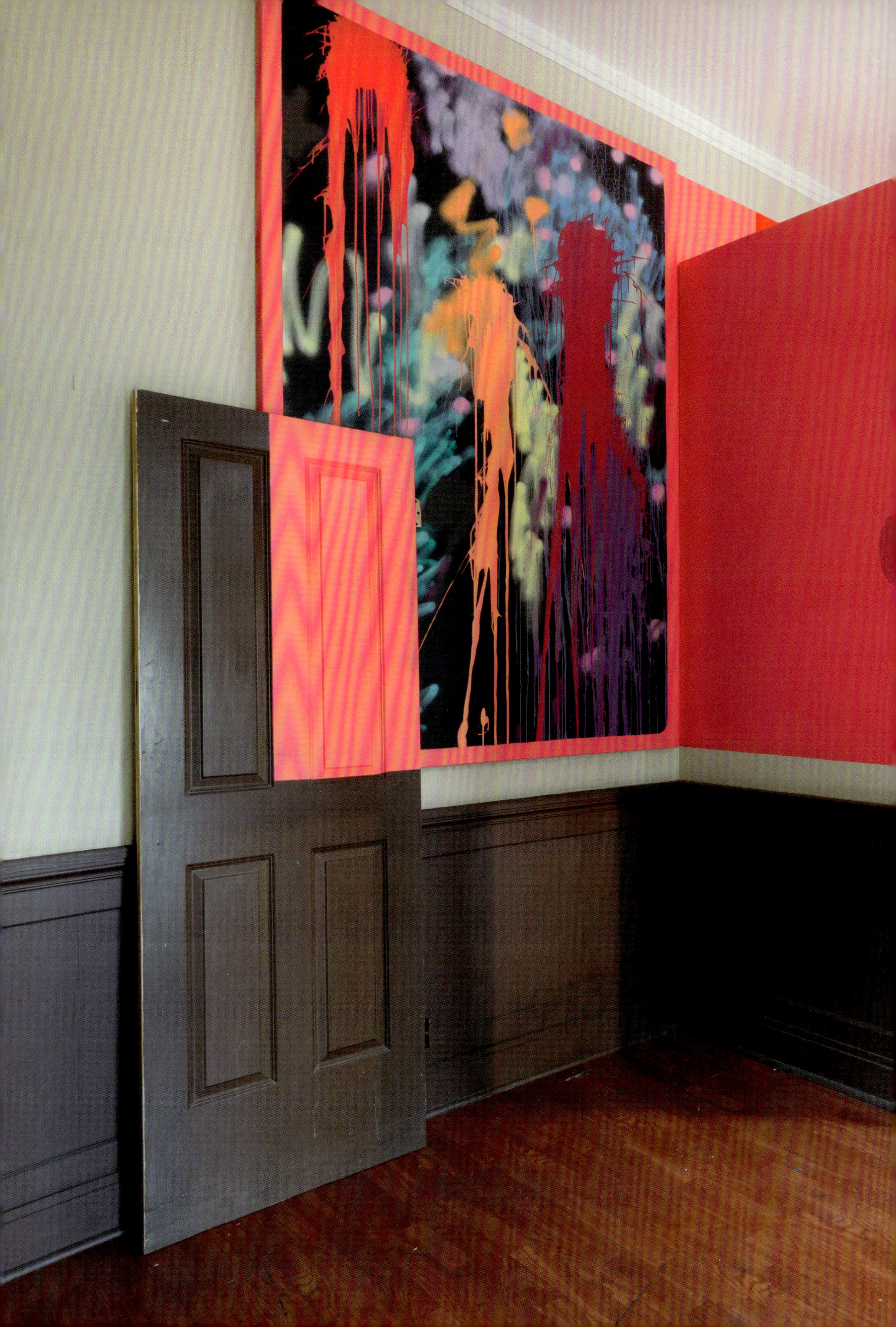

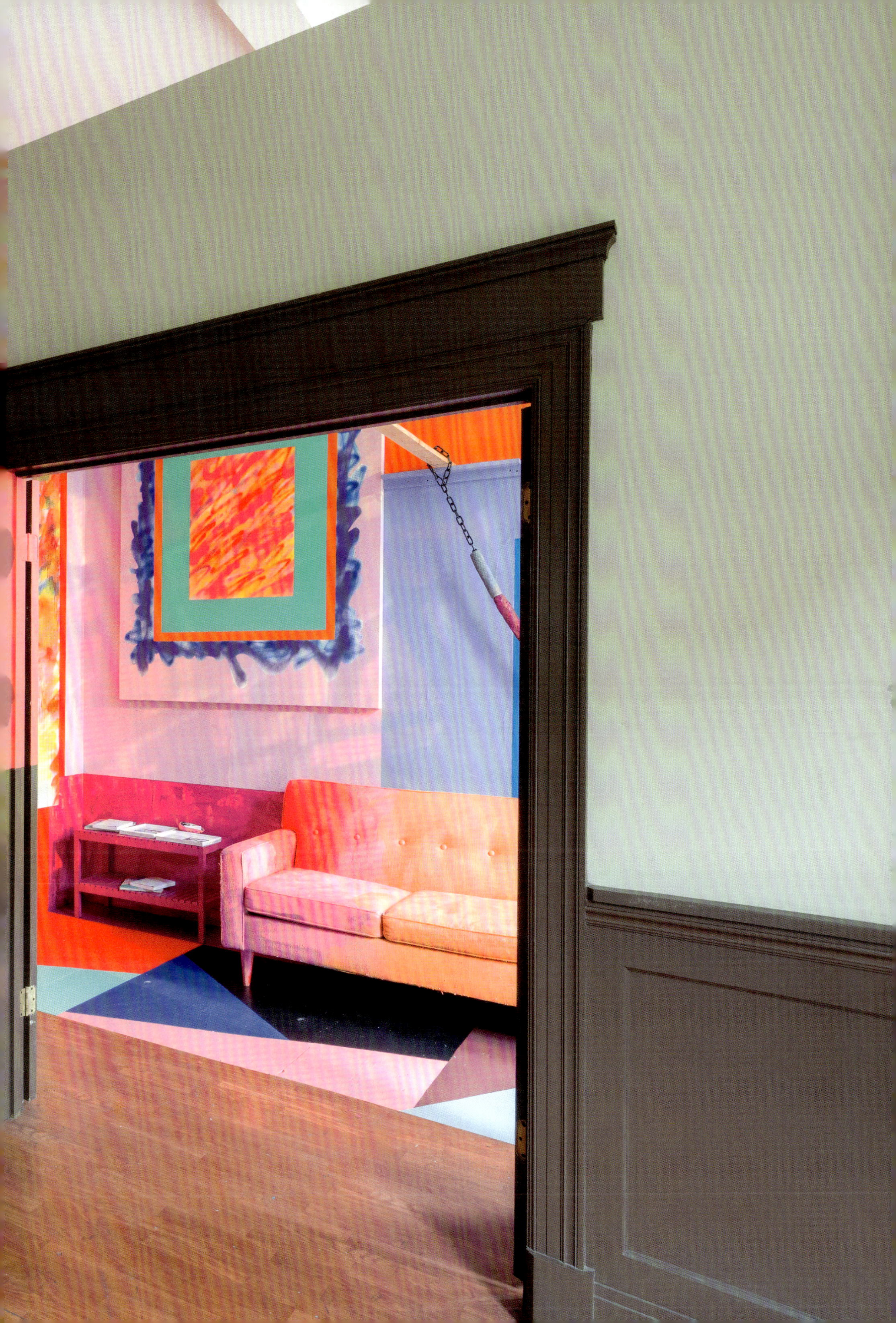

Ghosting, 2020

following spreads, **We Will Walk Right Up To The Sun**,
San Francisco International Airport, 2019

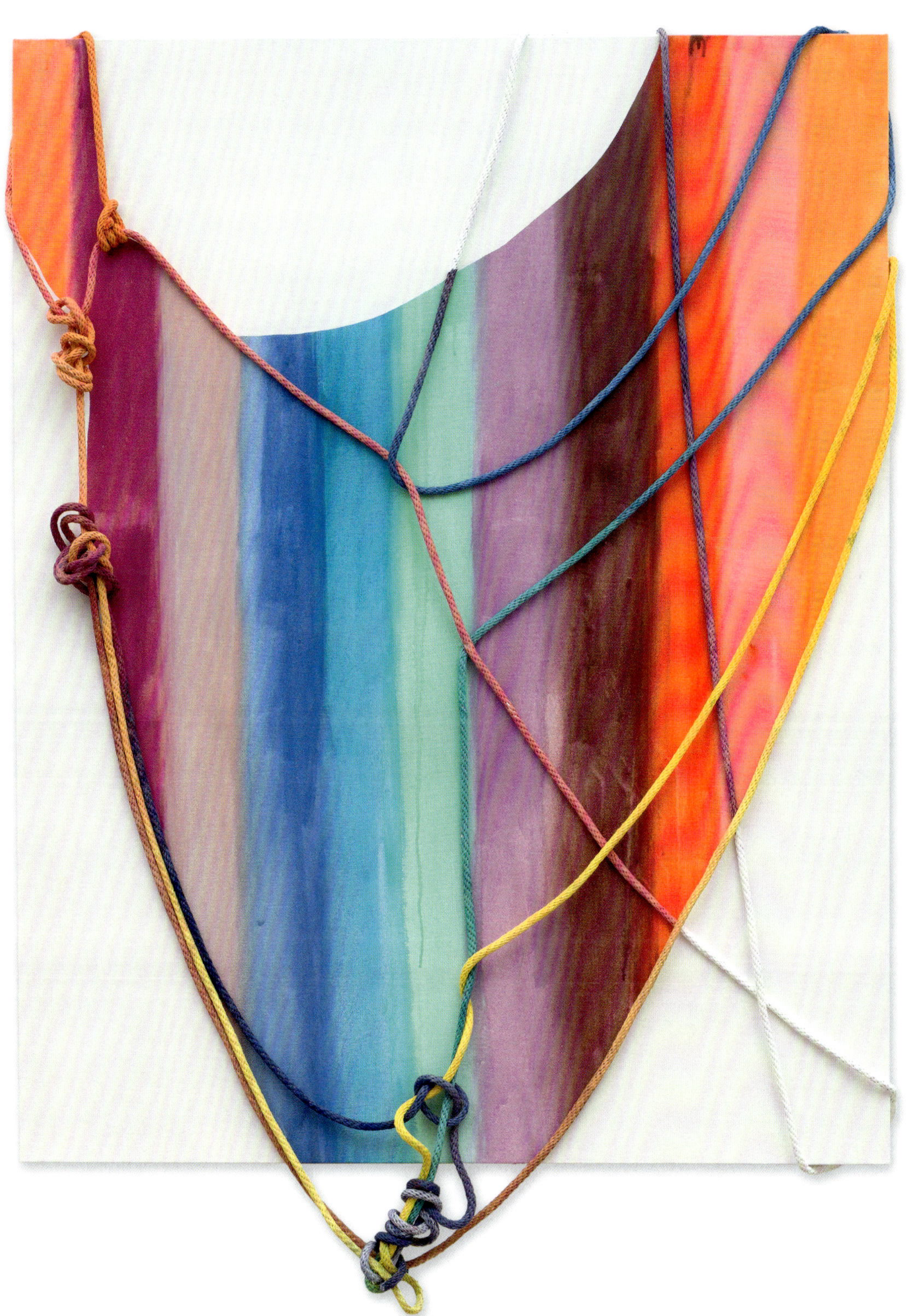

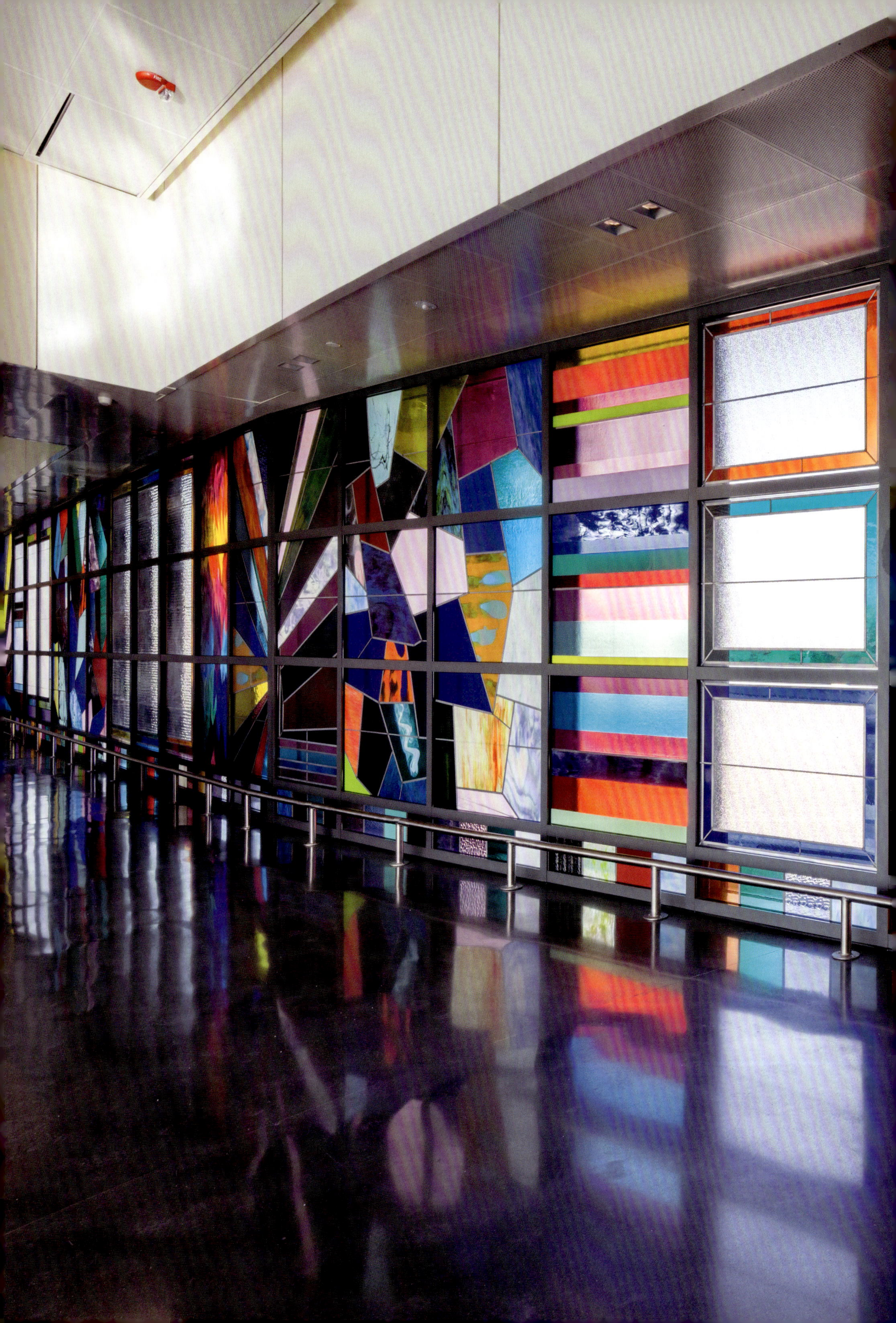

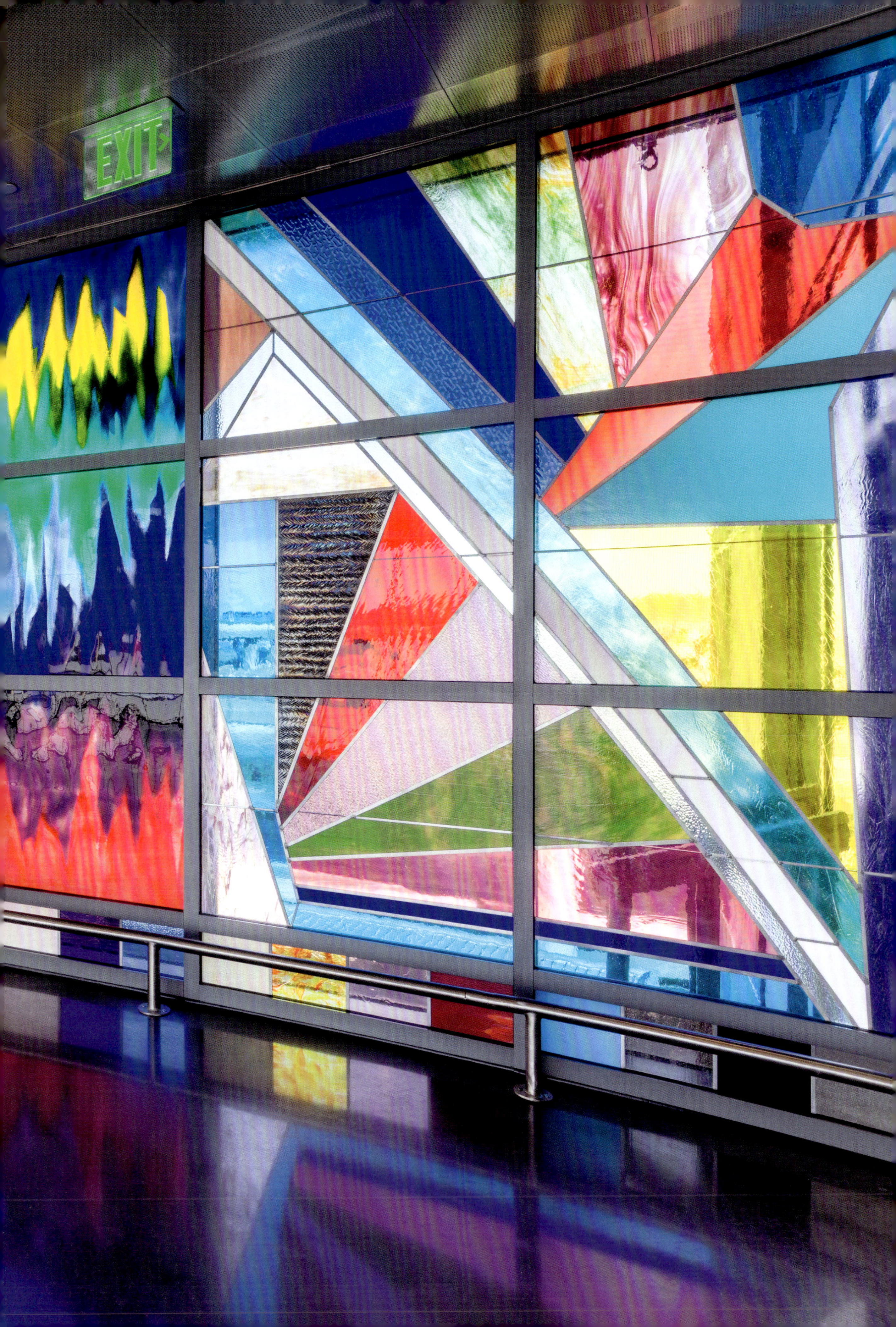

EXIT

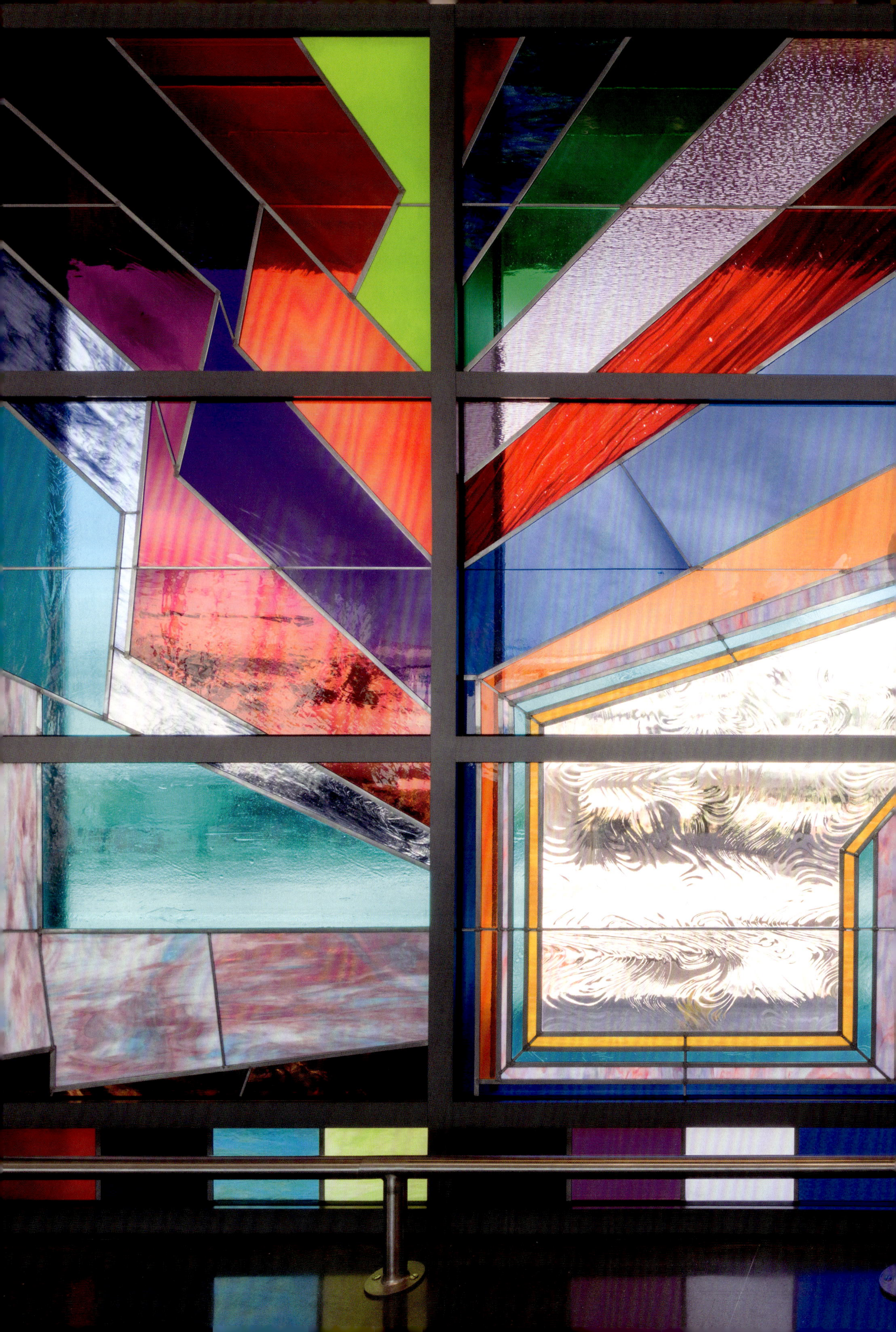

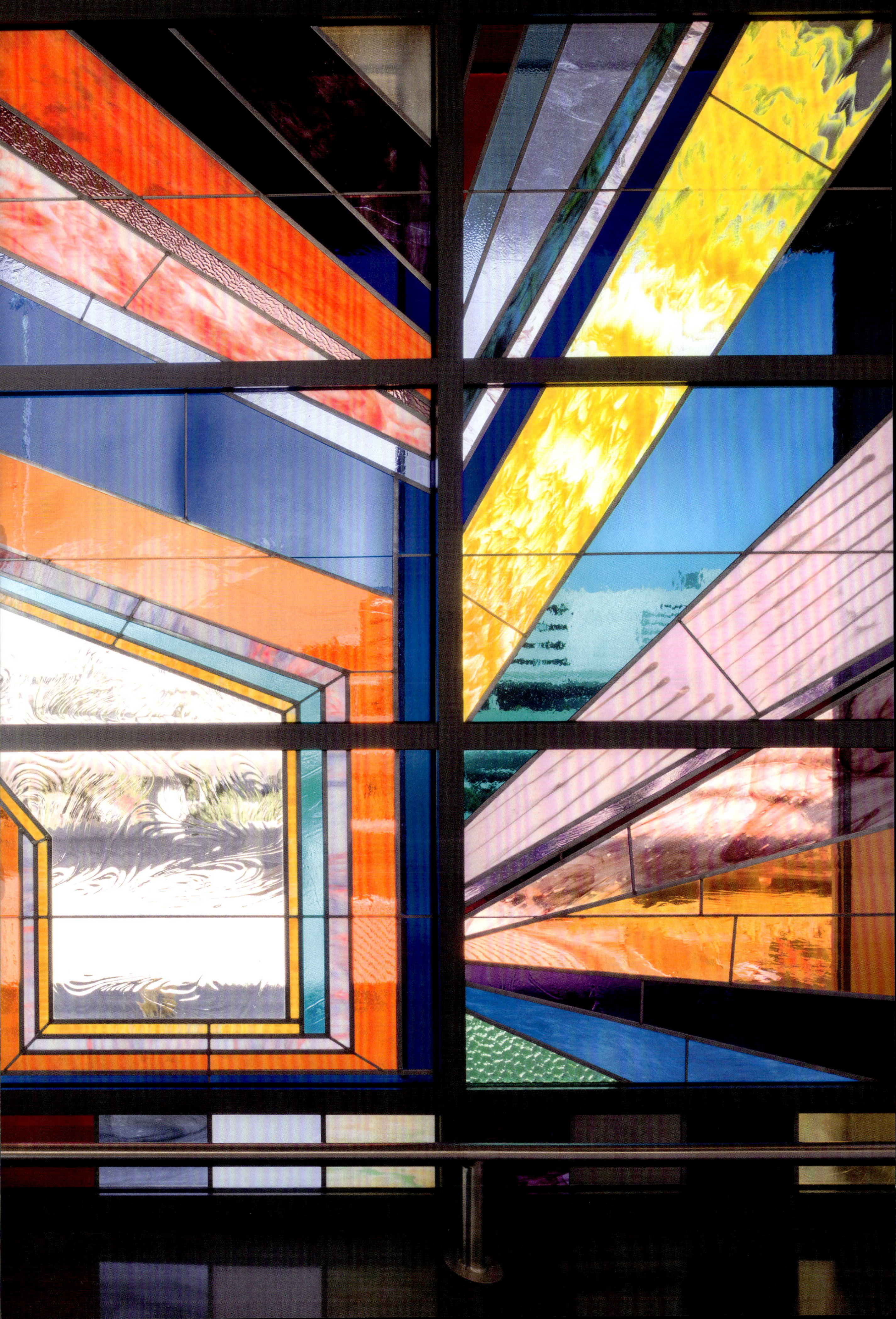

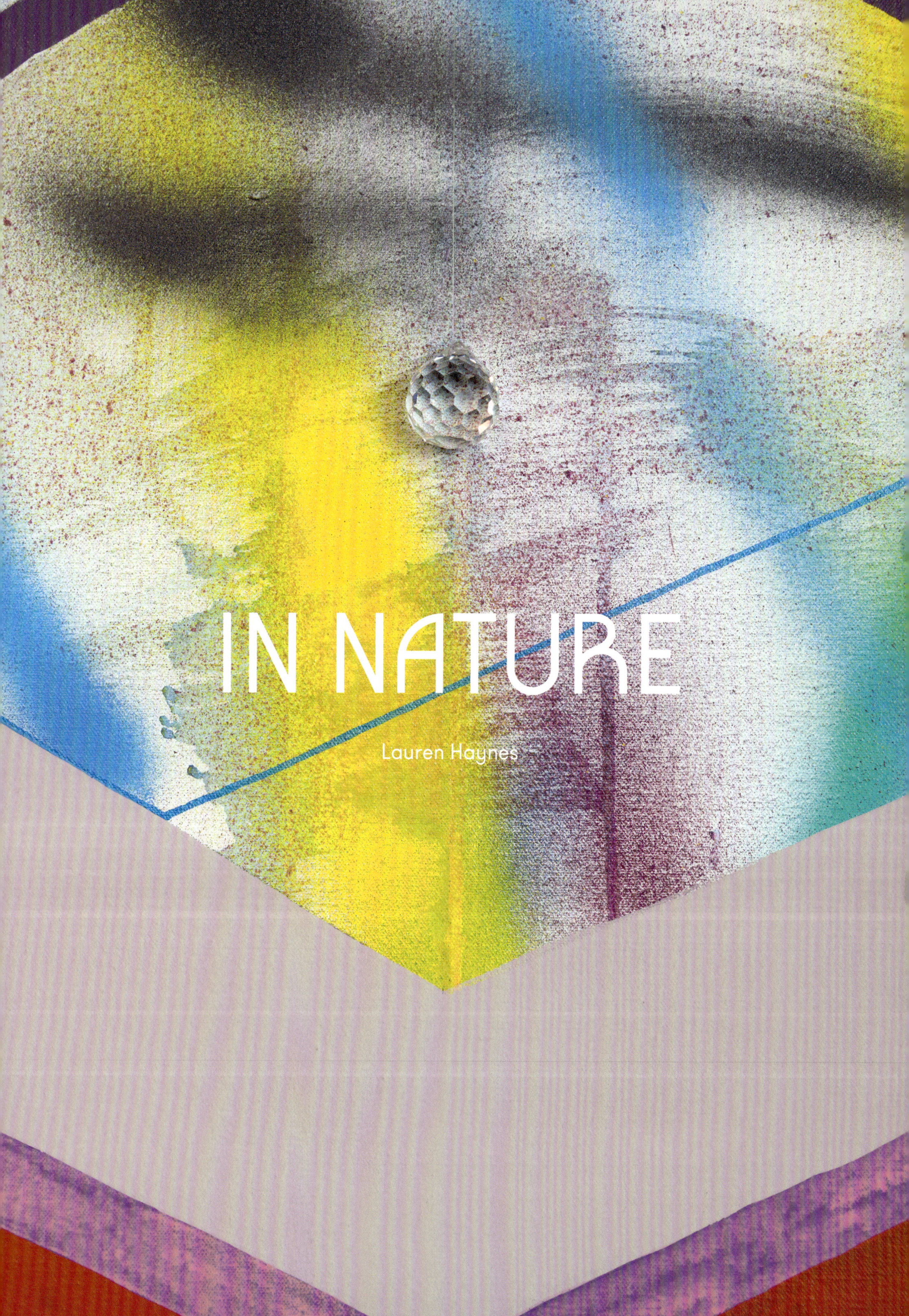
IN NATURE
Lauren Haynes

It is an understatement to say that 2020 was a year full of the unexpected. Everything changed, including the way museums and artists prepared and collaborated on exhibitions. During this time, working with Sarah Cain on her exhibition at the Momentary, *Sarah Cain: In Nature* (February 13–May 30, 2021), we learned a lot about planning amid uncertainty and being delighted by the unexpected. The Momentary is a satellite space of Crystal Bridges Museum of American Art in Bentonville, Arkansas and is focused on contemporary art across visual and performing arts disciplines. The building it is housed in, was formerly a cheese processing plant and has retained much of the look and feel of its previous life after its transformation into an arts space.

Sarah and I started the conversation about what we had hoped would be a site-specific installation in the Lobby Gallery a few years before the space opened on February 20, 2020. She was among the very first artists to do a walkthrough while it was still under construction and thanks to those early site visits, Sarah was able to develop a plan for the space remotely. There were even some original architectural features that might not have been preserved had we not been working with her. It was exciting to see how *In Nature* evolved given limitations on travel and access to spaces and materials. Instead of a site-specific installation, what developed was more of a site-responsive project that included both newly created and repurposed artworks. Sarah produced a floor painting for the Momentary by recreating the layout of the Lobby Gallery in her studio in California. Her use of color, space and interest in abstraction are all at the forefront of *In Nature*.

On the occasion of *Sarah Cain: In Nature*, Sarah and I had a conversation to document the moment and the project. Some highlights of that conversation are included here.

◊◊◊

LAUREN HAYNES: How do you start thinking about a site-specific exhibition like *In Nature?*

SARAH CAIN: **Usually it starts with a site visit so I can get the feel and flow of the space, as well as the context and environment outside. I collect details that could be random—like something I see or smell in the space. My process is fluid; I change things a lot. This is what working on site is about—letting go of control, being present, making something that is active instead of just an object that sits.**

What were some of your first impressions of the Momentary and Northwest Arkansas?

One of my strongest memories from my first walkthrough at the Momentary, before it was finished, was the smell of milk. I loved the rawness of the space. I was also struck by the vast landscape around the site. It felt particular and connected to the interior ruggedness of the building. There was a sense of freedom and the possibilities felt sort of endless.

We started the conversation about your doing a project here a couple of years ago and we always planned for you to come and create onsite. How did your process for developing *In Nature* change due to the pandemic and travel restrictions?

It changed a lot. I had to shift all of the works that I was going to make on-site, to works that I created mostly in my studio and then adapted or regrouped on-site. For example, I considered the idea of pulling one of the hanging canvas works through an existing hole in the Lobby Gallery, so I had to measure it out and make a fake hole in my studio.

It was much more work than my typical approach of stressing-out and then just busting the work out in two weeks. I'm learning a new sense of time and techniques of making in the studio, which I probably wouldn't have if I didn't have to. It's amazing to me how long everything is taking. Even though I fight the idea of a museum feeling like a mausoleum, I do want my work to survive me.

How are the individual pieces of the exhibition connected for you? How do they make one installation, one complete work?

They're connected by the theme of nature, which is one of my main inspirations, pandemic or not. I grew up on a dirt road so it's one of the things that really grounds me. There are studies that show that if you look at trees for thirty minutes a day, your brain chemistry changes. When I was working on this exhibition, I was thinking about the small things we can do to make ourselves okay.

How did you come up with the title *In Nature*?

In Nature ties into the basic relationship to nature that is at the core of looking, which in turn, might be at the core of painting. Joan Mitchell and Celia Paul both say that nature was their main inspiration. The act of sitting in nature is very similar to sitting in the painting studio—being open, waiting, letting your thoughts move through you until you get into a state that's close to meditation. My whole life, I've always just walked in the woods, through a field, to the creek to sit and wait to see what happens. If my practice were in nature, it'd be the wild side of a garden.

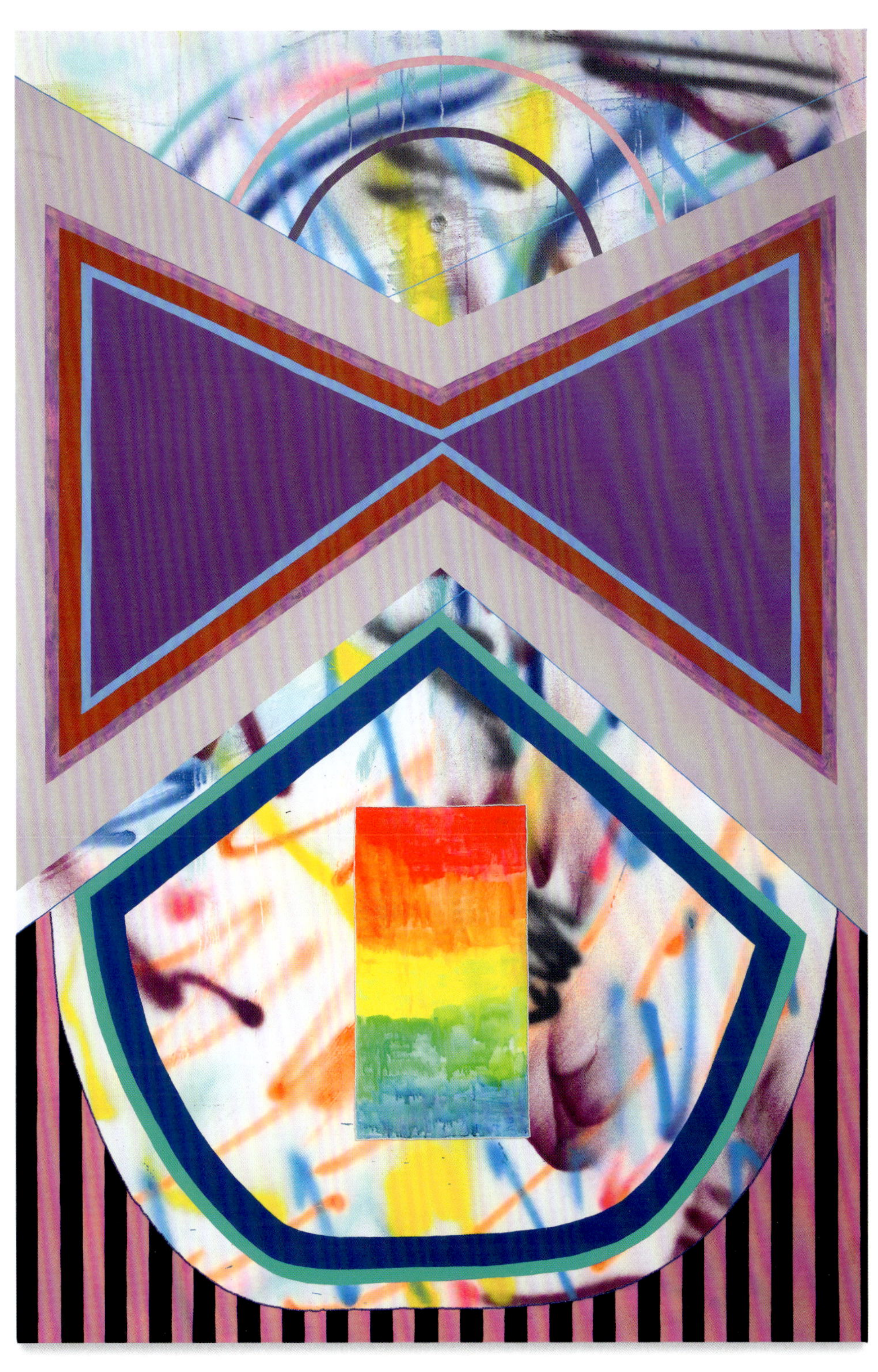

Black Widow, 2018
(detail on page 108)

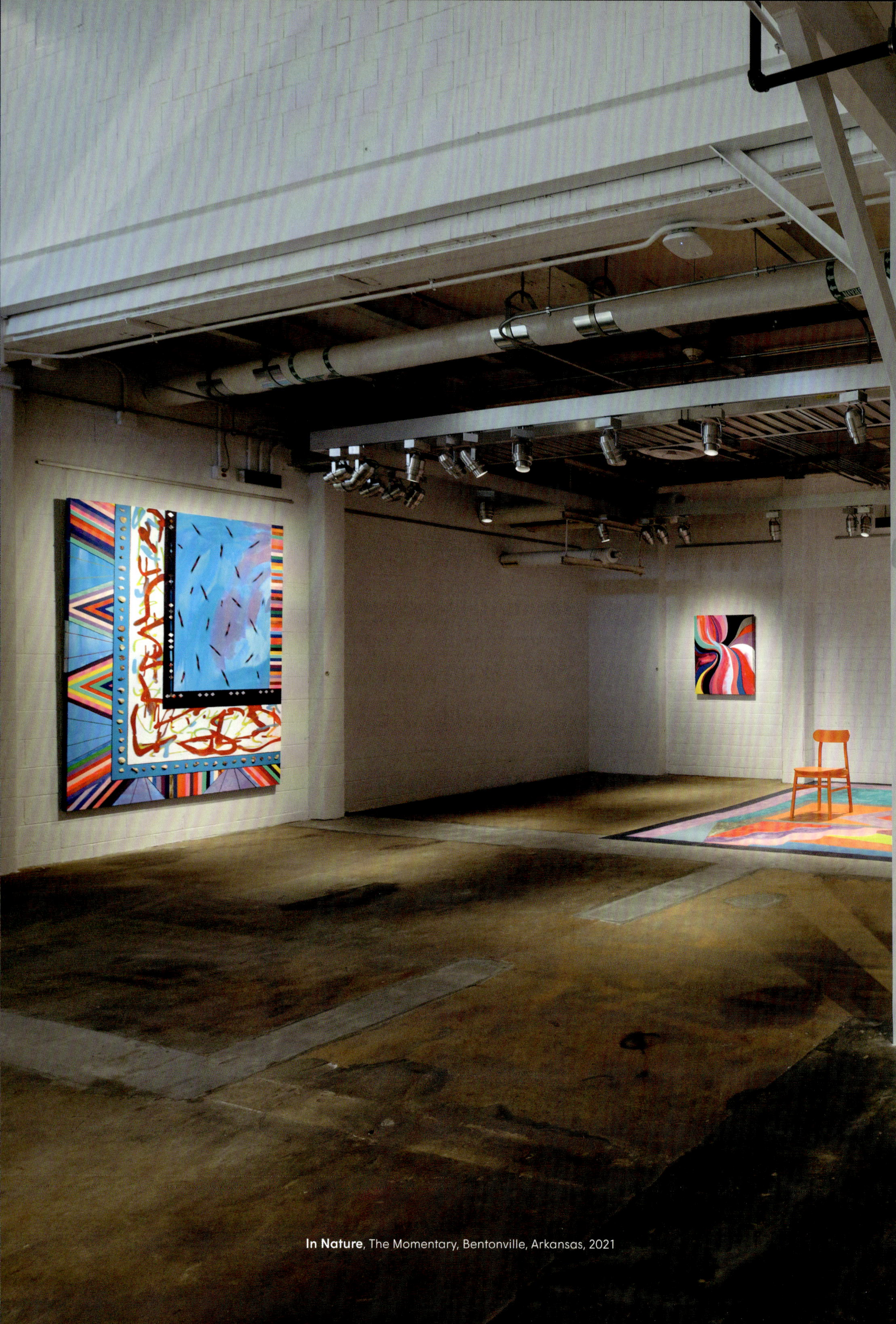

In Nature, The Momentary, Bentonville, Arkansas, 2021

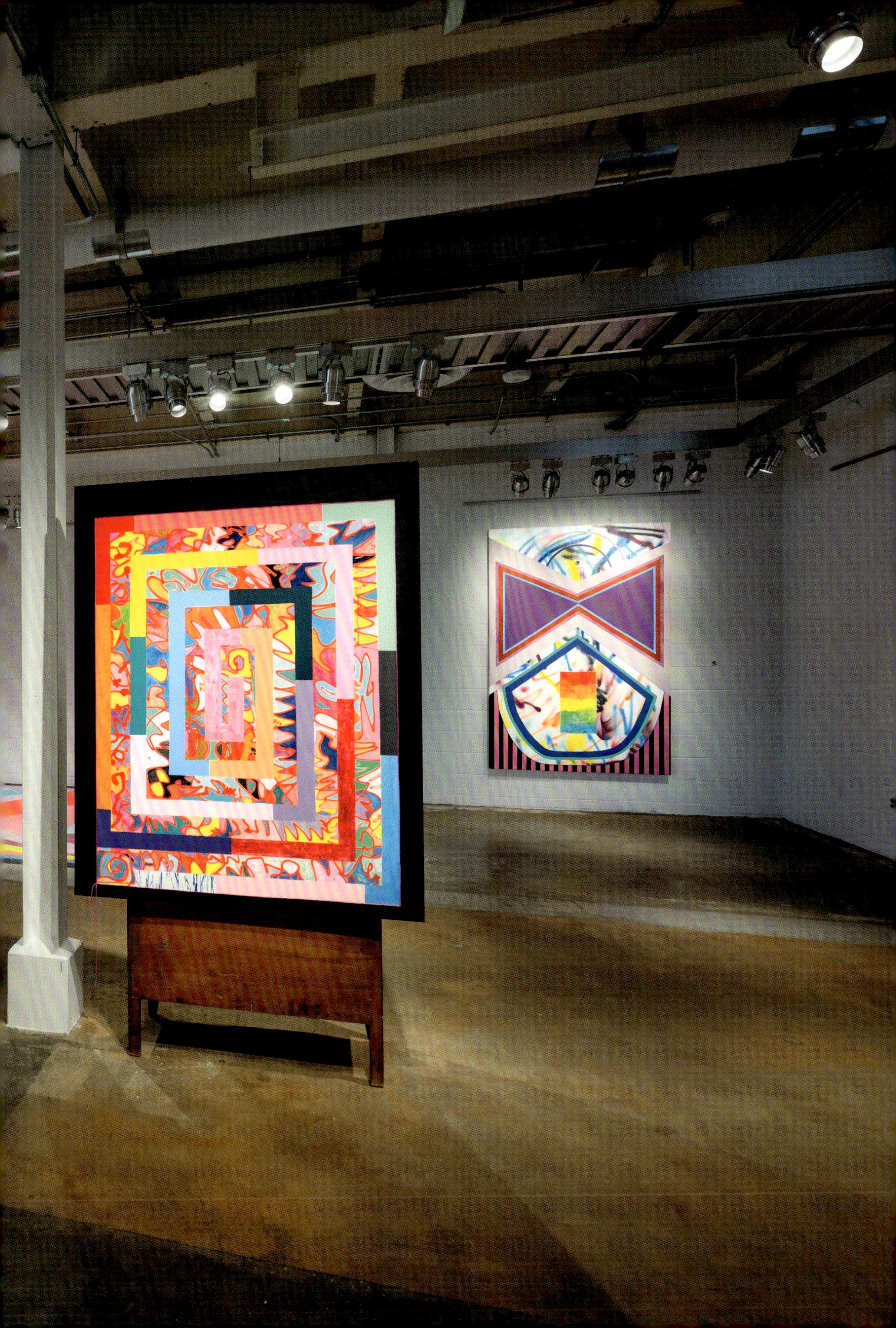

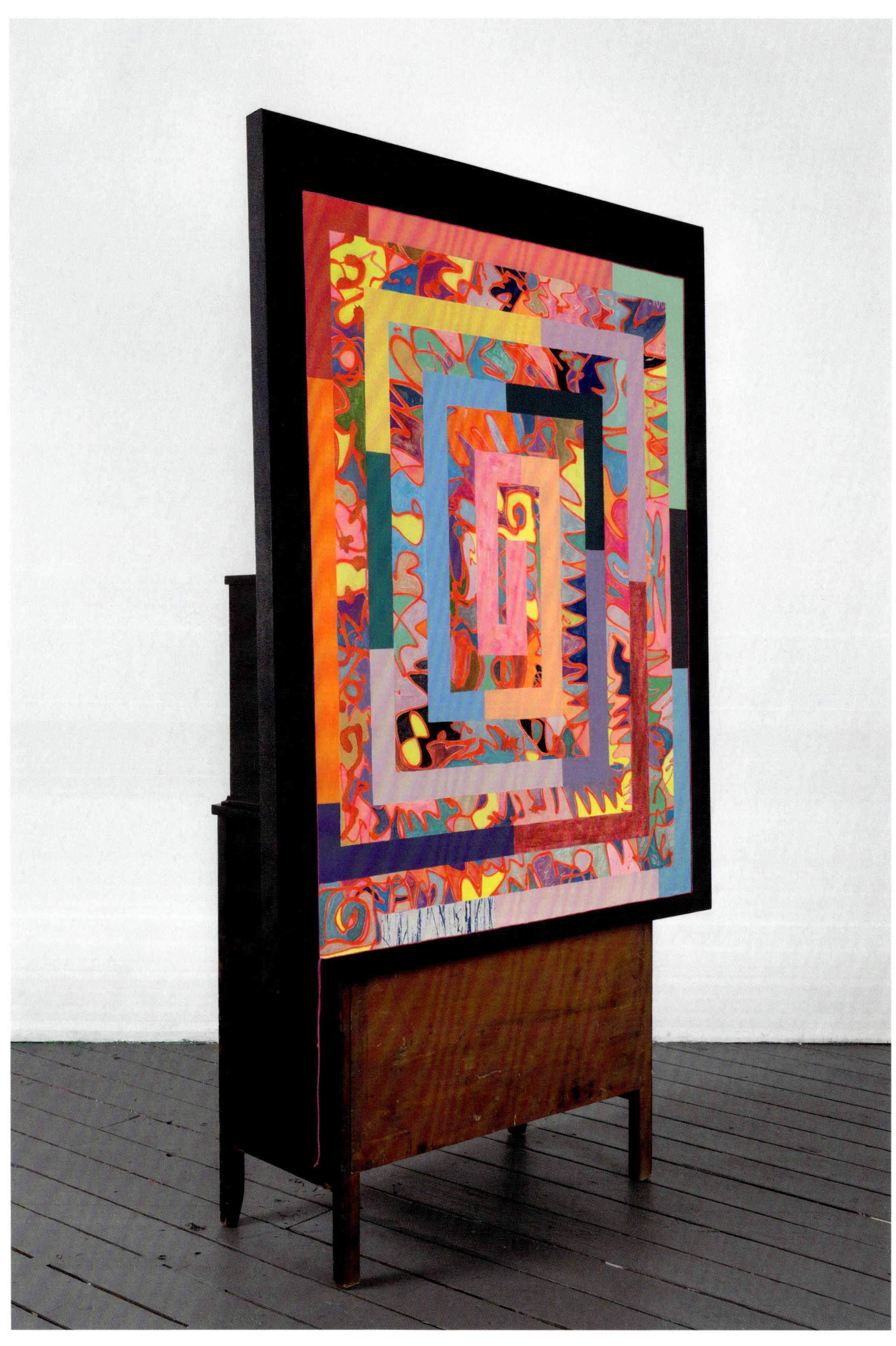

(Untitled) dresser, 2015

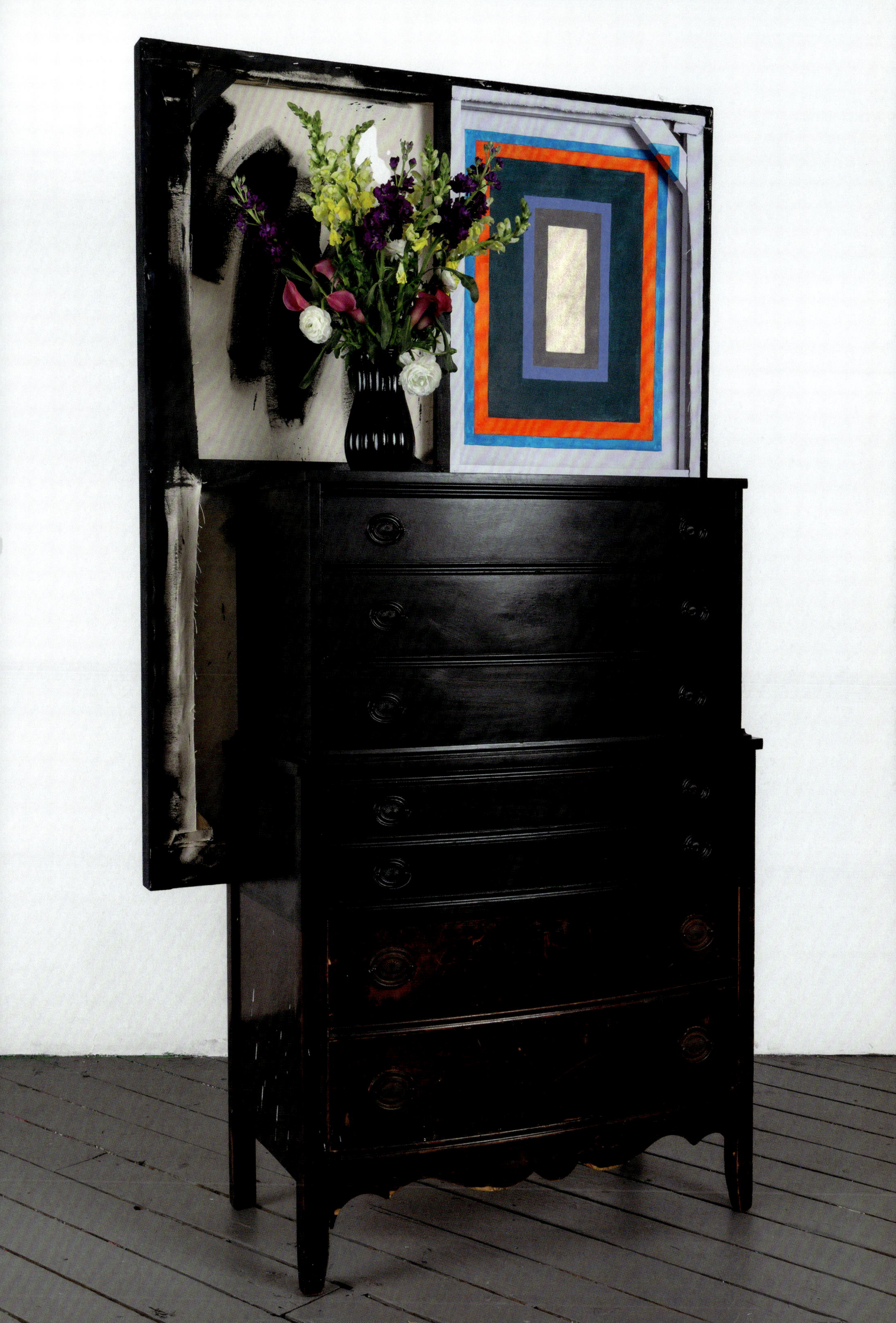

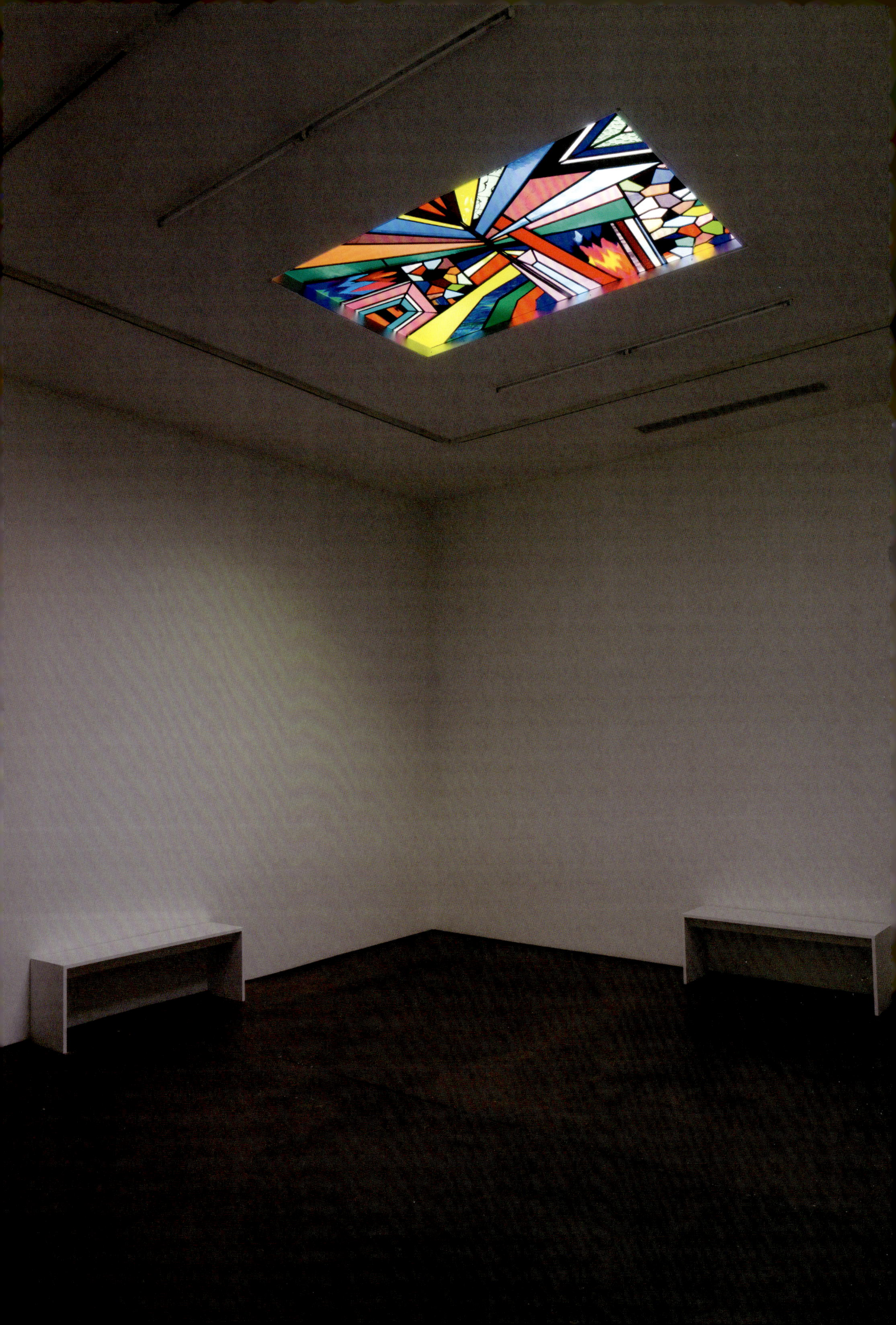

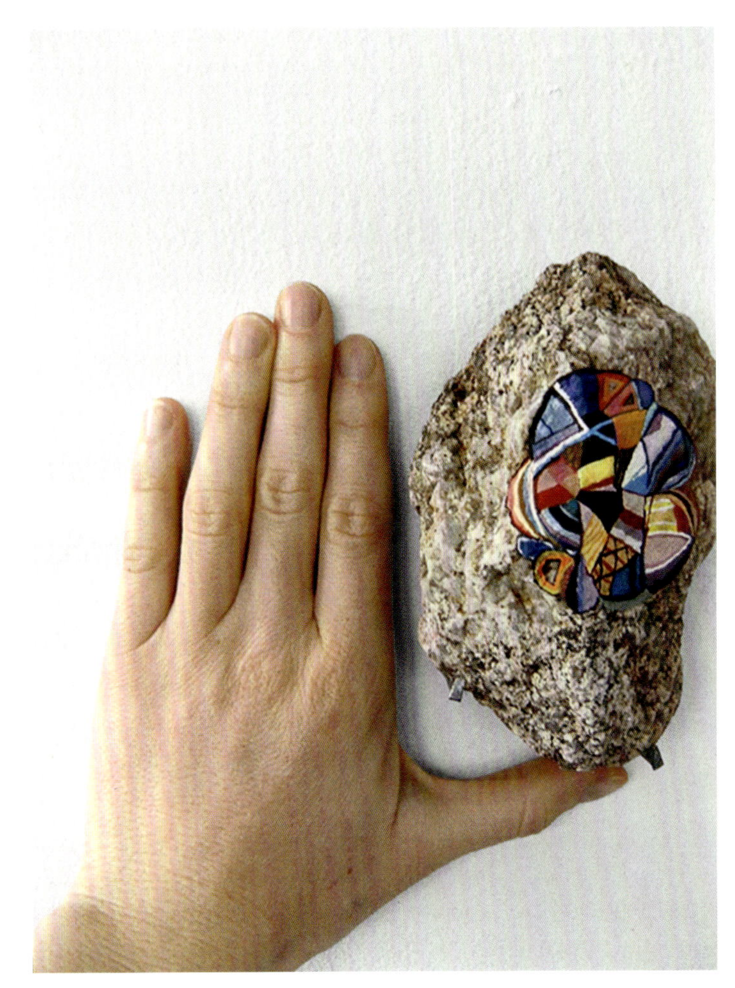

Rock of good will, 2005

facing, **The Sun Will Not Wait (skylight)**, 2019

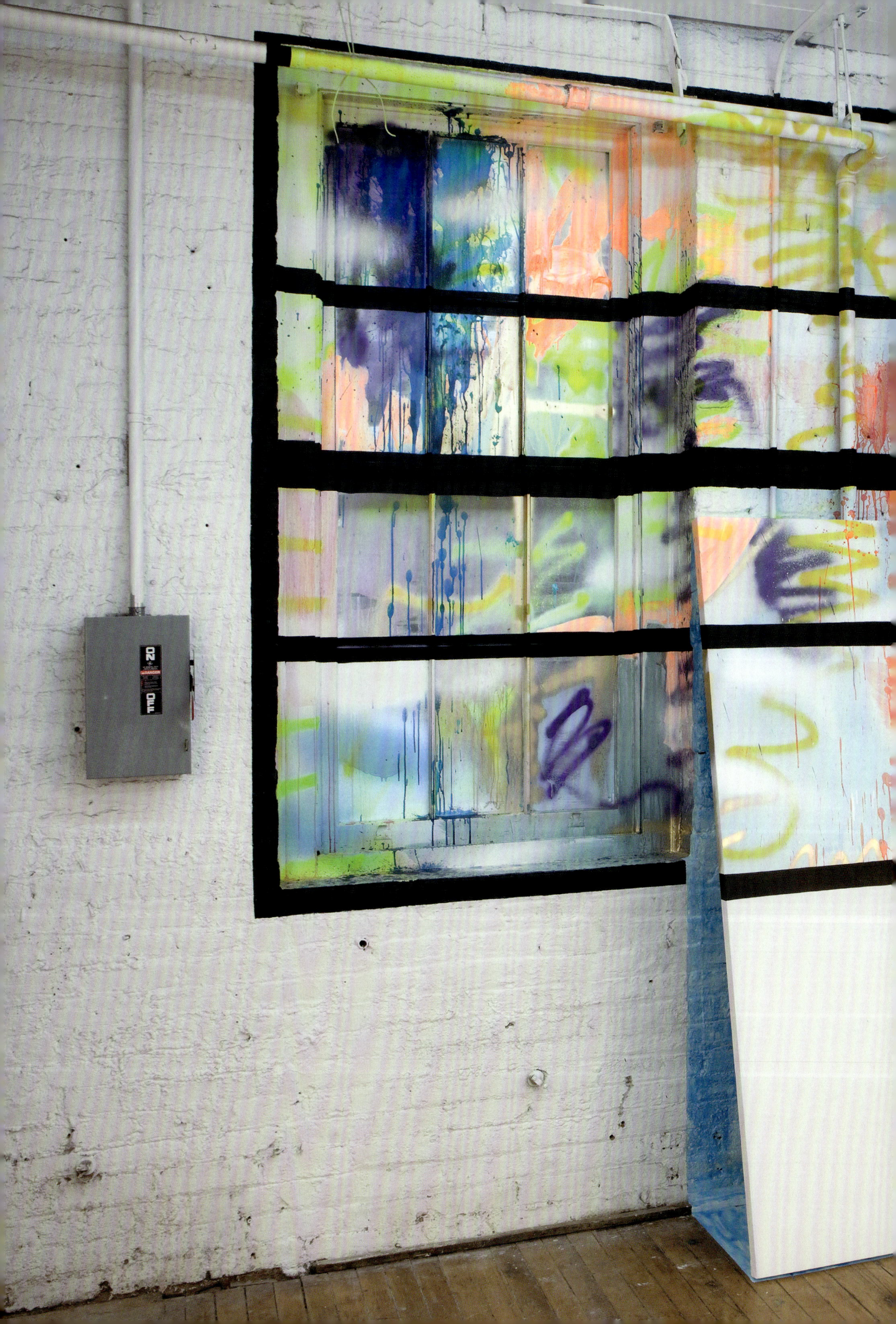

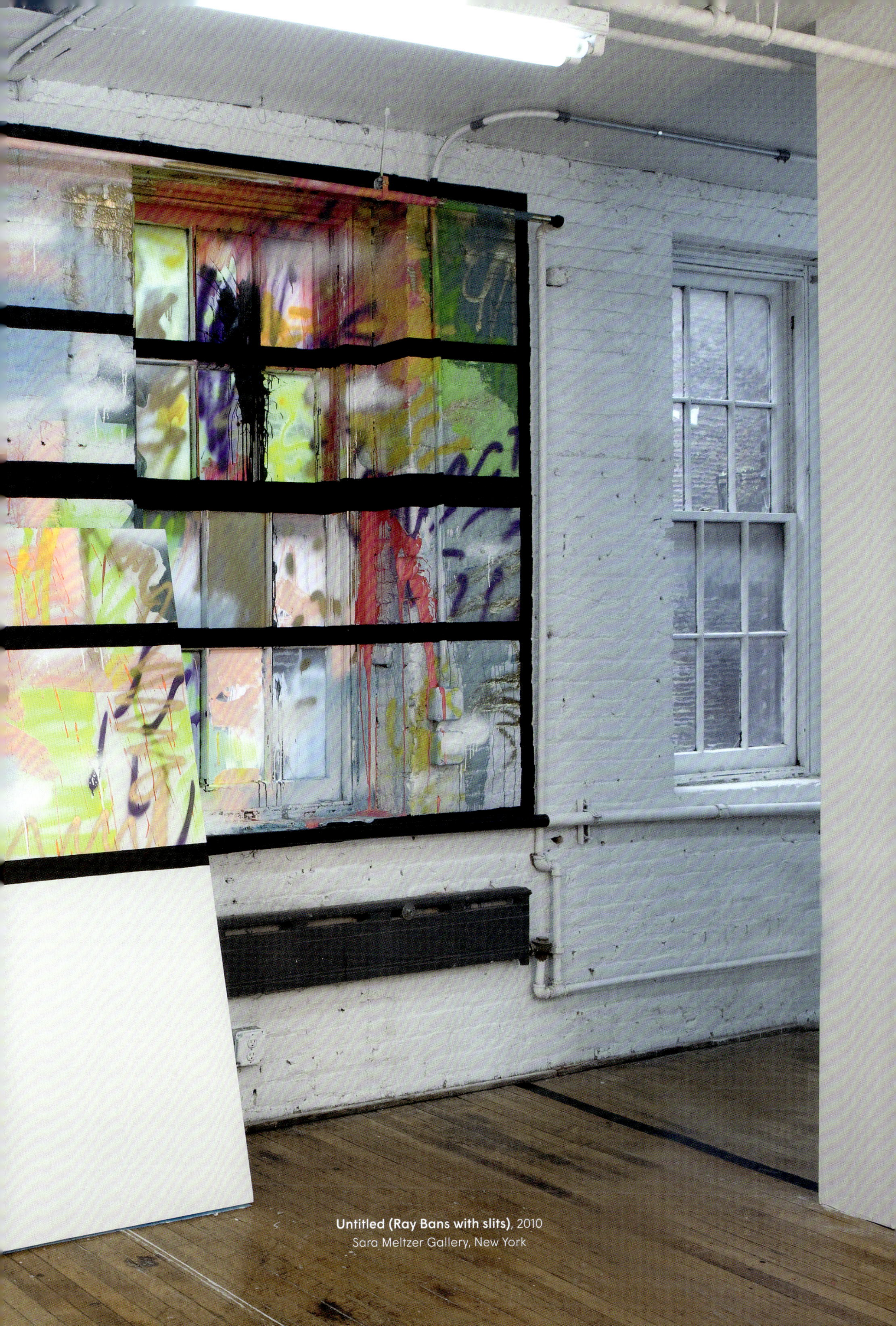

Untitled (Ray Bans with slits), 2010
Sara Meltzer Gallery, New York

following spread, **Enter the Center**, Tang Teaching Museum at
Skidmore College, Saratoga Springs, New York, 2021

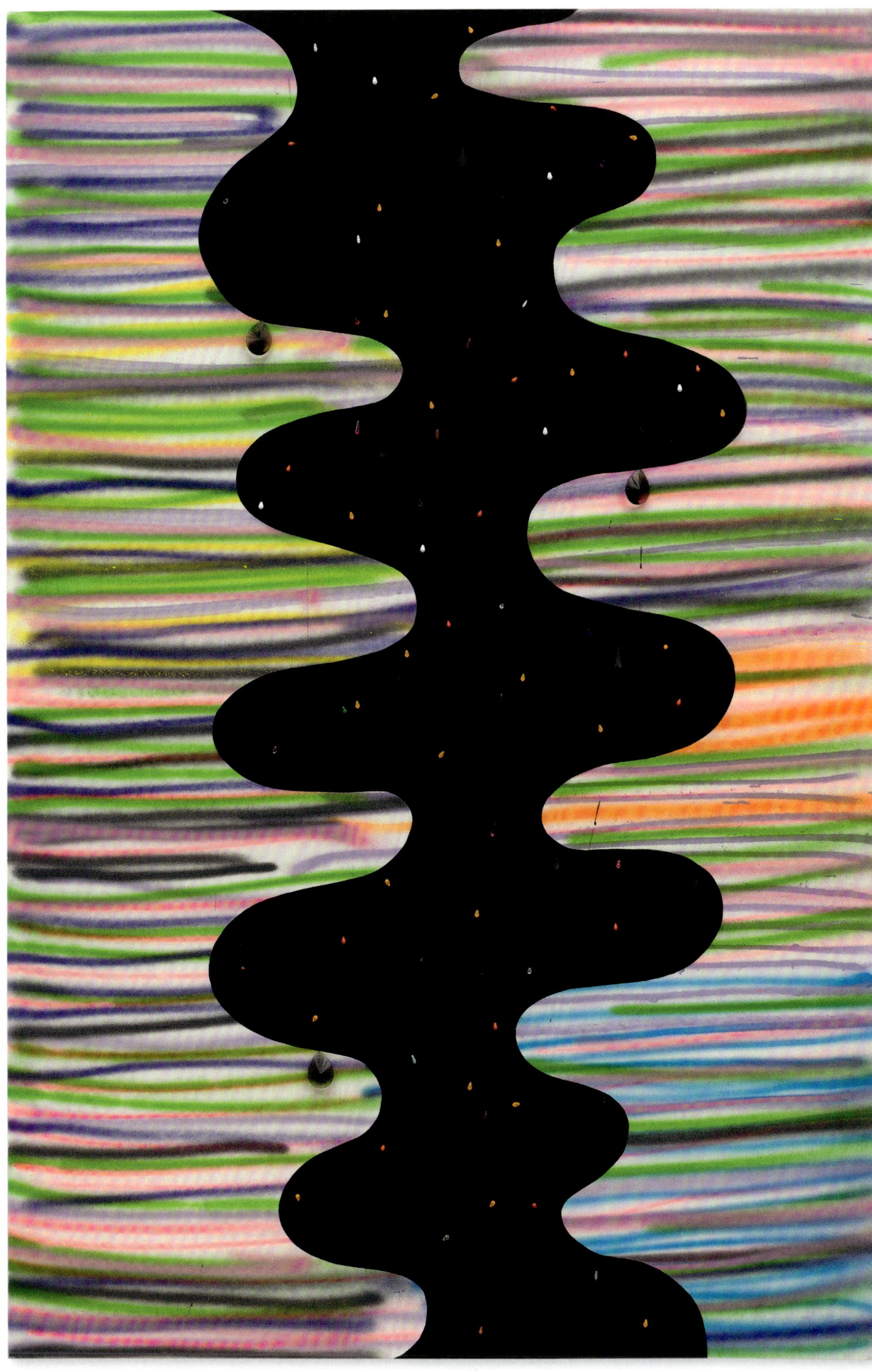

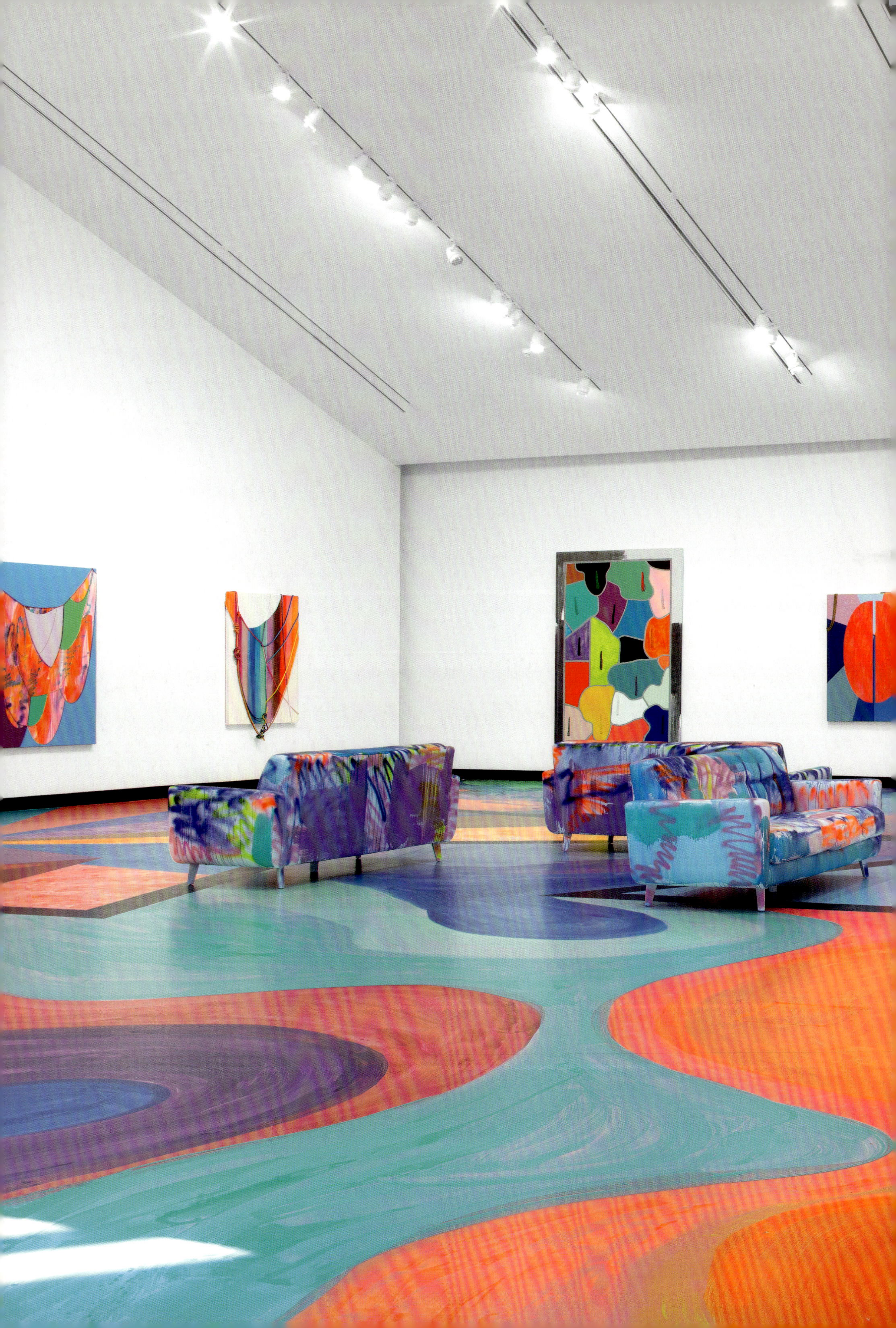

Published on the occasion of the exhibition

Opener 33

SARAH CAIN—ENTER THE CENTER

Curated by Ian Berry in collaboration with the artist

The Frances Young Tang Teaching Museum and
Art Gallery at Skidmore College
July 10–December 19, 2021

First edition published June 2022 by The Frances
Young Tang Teaching Museum and Art Gallery,
Skidmore College, Saratoga Springs, New York, and
DelMonico Books, New York

The Frances Young Tang Teaching Museum and
Art Gallery at Skidmore College
815 N. Broadway
Saratoga Springs, NY 12866
tang.skidmore.edu

DelMonico Books available through
ARTBOOK | D.A.P.
75 Broad Street, Suite 630
New York, NY 10004
artbook.com
delmonicobooks.com

ISBN: 978-1-63681-014-0
Library of Congress Control Number: 2022940159

Design by Beverly Joel, pulp, ink.
Color separations by ARTPRODUCT, Los Angeles
Printed by Conti Tipocolor, Firenze

Sarah Cain: Enter the Center is made possible with
generous support from Iris Zurawin Marden '71.

The catalogue is made possible with support from
Kiki and Zach McMillan.

The Opener Series is supported by the New York
State Council on the Arts, Ann Schapps Schaffer '62
and Mel Schaffer, Beverly Beatson Grossman '58,
and Friends of the Tang.

Thanks to all photographers whose work is
featured in this book including:
Pages 1, 2, 4, 6, 9, 30–31, 33, 35, 36, 37, 39, 41, 42–43,
44, 48–49, 53, 56, 57, 65, 66–67, 74, 75, 81, 124–125, 136:
Arthur Evans
Page 10, 20, 119: Sarah Cain
Page 11: Courtesy Orange County Museum of Art,
photo by Colin Young-Wolff
Pages 15, 16, 17, 18–19, 25, 27, 29, 54–55, 57, 69, 71,
72–73, 77, 78, 79, 81, 82–83, 84–85, 86–87, 89, 98, 99, 100,
102–103, 105, 106–107, 108–109, 110, 113, 118 123:
Jeff McClane
Pages 22–23: Courtesy Galerie Lelong
Page 61, 63, 88, 116–117: Joshua White
Page 114–115: Ironside photography

Front cover:
bras, 2017 (detail)
Acrylic, beads, bras, spray paint on canvas
72 × 60 inches
Collection of Jennifer and Stephen Maguire

Back cover:
Self Portrait, 2020 (detail)
Acrylic, gouache, latex, prism beads, plastic thread
90 × 90 × 3 inches
Collection of the National Gallery of Art, Washington
DC, purchased as a Gift of Sharon Percy Rockefeller
and Senator John Davison Rockefeller IV

CONTRIBUTORS

Ian Berry is Dayton Director of The Frances Young
Tang Teaching Museum and Art Gallery and Professor
of Liberal Arts at Skidmore College.

Sarah Cain is an artist based in Los Angeles.

Andy Campbell is a writer and Associate Professor of
Critical Studies at USC - Roski School of Art and Design
in Los Angeles.

Lauren Haynes is Director of Curatorial Affairs and
Programs at the Queens Museum.

Bernadette Mayer is a poet, writer, and visual artist.

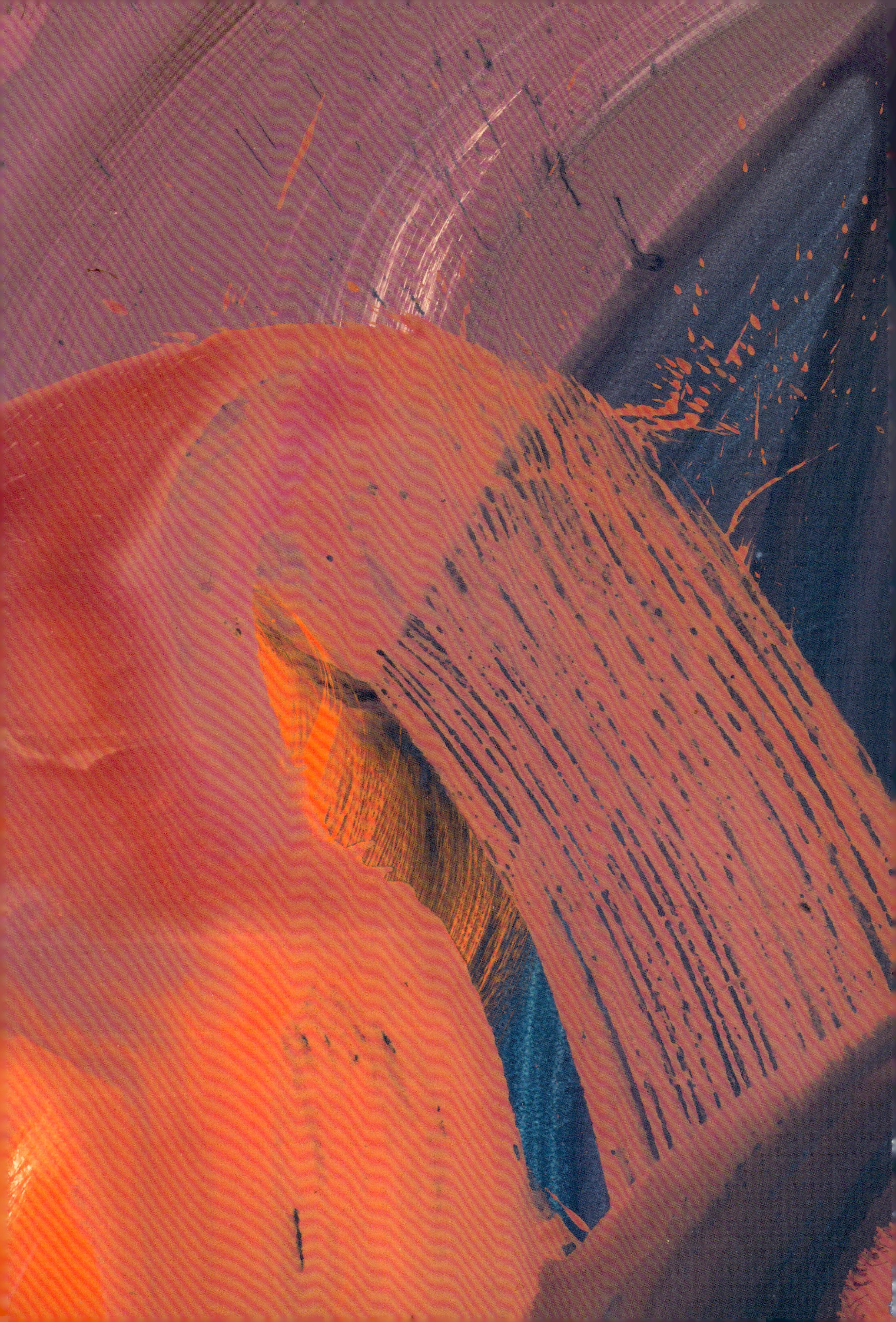